FIREWORKS

FIREWORKS

Jerry Ryan in
Commonweal

Edited and with a Foreword by
PATRICK JORDAN

www.commonwealmagazine.org

Commonweal
475 Riverside Drive
Room 405
New York, NY 10115
212-662-4200
commonwealmagazine.org

Cover design and book layout by David Sankey.

ISBN 978-0-578-75608-0

For Nayda and Steven

CONTENTS

Last (and Lasting) Things

FOREWORD

Although Jerry Ryan (1937-2020) was born in Boston, attended high school and college there, and spent his last forty years in the area, he was anything but provincial. The son of working-class Irish and Lithuanian parents, he became a top student at Boston College, before spending his middle years working with the poor and disenfranchised in Europe and South America. Most of those years were as a member of the Little Brothers of Jesus, a Roman Catholic community dedicated to exemplifying the life and spirituality of Charles de Foucauld (1858-1916). The Little Brothers lead a hidden life: praying in common, while living among the poor and sharing their work. As a result, Jerry came to experience the vicissitudes of life on the knife's edge. A keen observer of the world's injustice and the church's indifference, he responded by attempting to live out Catholic social teaching on a daily basis.

Jerry Ryan had a sense of self-deprecating humor and he shared a rejuvenating comradery with his fellow workers, whether in factories, graveyards, or in a ship's engine room. He knew their sense of precarity and was often chosen to represent them before those in power. His quick, subtle mind enabled him to evaluate situations and suggest possible solutions. These same qualities were evident in Jerry's journalism in such publications as *Commonweal, America, National Catholic Reporter,* and the *Catholic Worker.* Further, he had a rich and substantial theological background. Schooled by French Dominicans on the eve of Vatican II, his innate exploratory bent and attention to substance never failed him. Coupled with this theological understanding and a no-nonsense take on history—past and present—Jerry communicated the most subtle and evocative truths of the Christian faith in readily understandable, accessible language. Fluent in French and Spanish (he translated theological works from both into English), he incorporated these insights into his writing.

Jerry Ryan left the Little Brothers in 1978. He had witnessed and written about the Chilean coup of 1973, been forced to flee the country for his life, and had relocated to Bolivia. There he met Nayda Madrid. They married in 1978 and had a son, Steven. After a series of military coups in Bolivia, in 1980 Jerry and his family settled in Boston. It was there Jerry found work for thirty-three years as a custodian and shop steward at the New England Aquarium. He retired at the age of seventy-seven, following a work-related fall. Fortunately, none of this hampered his writing—which continued until his death—and allowed him to further explore other religious traditions, enriching and deepening his Catholic faith and understanding.

This collection of Jerry Ryan's *Commonweal* articles—thirty-two pieces written over nearly fifty years—is divided into four loosely thematic (not chronological) sections. They deal with what might be called his "basics," "explorations and experience," "encounters with otherness," and "diminishment and rising." In all of his writing, Jerry engaged the Christian mysteries in their wondrous depth and subtlety, yet always through the lens of his own adventuresome, courageous, and exemplary life.

—Patrick Jordan

Heart of
the Matter

FIREWORKS

For perhaps ten years, on the evening before every Fourth of July, there were fireworks over Boston Harbor synchronized with Handel's "Royal Hymn to Fireworks." When this piece was first composed to celebrate the peace treaty that put an end to the War of the Austrian Succession, the fireworks were just the background for the music. In Boston, they were the main event. I always had a front-row seat. At the time I was working the second shift (3 to 11 p.m.) at the New England Aquarium, on a barge where the sea lions and dolphins were lodged. The band played on a patio alongside the aquarium barge, while the fireworks barge sat in the harbor just behind the aquarium. It doesn't get much better than that.

The whole spectacle was breathtakingly beautiful. The fireworks were perfectly in sync with the music. Smoke would linger with a sustained note. Small, discreet, but extremely graceful fireworks represented the softer, slower parts. The crescendos swept you up with them. Once, as I watched and listened, it occurred to me that this was perhaps the most beautiful manmade spectacle I had ever seen.

It didn't last. People didn't appreciate it—though maybe if they had had my seat they would have. The aquarium barge had a function room on the top deck, and the week before the Fourth the band would come aboard to practice there. I happened to be passing by when one of the rehearsals was breaking up and noticed a woman who had a piccolo in her hand and seemed rather lost. I thought maybe I could cheer her up by telling her how wonderful I thought the show was, and how grateful I was that she was helping to make it happen. She replied, a little sadly, that she wasn't able to see the fireworks because everyone in the orchestra had their backs to the harbor. And, anyway, her whole attention was focused on not making any big mistakes in her piccolo part.

For some reason, that reply impressed me deeply. Aren't most of us in a similar situation? We are locked up in our own little worlds, trying not to get hurt too much or screw things up too badly, and we have our backs to the fireworks going on all around us, to all the activity of the saints, the whole household of God, with the angels and the patriarchs, the prophets and the martyrs, the virgins and apostles—the festal gathering of all those who've accepted the Divine Mercy, who have buried the dead, fed the hungry, and wiped the tears of the sorrowful. The fireworks ascend in various displays of glory and then silently descend as wisps of smoke, symbols of grace. It's like Jacob's dream of the ladder between heaven and earth and God's messengers continually descending and ascending. And there is the mysterious presence of all those whom we have known and loved, who have made us what we are, with whom we're linked forever.

I wish I had thought of this in time to tell the piccolo player, whose name I never knew and whom I never saw again. But, as so often happens with me, I thought of what I should have said too late. I should also have told her that, even though she couldn't see what was going on around her, her piccolo role was very important: without it, something would have been lacking in the spectacle. We must play our part without (yet) knowing its whole significance.

July 5, 2019

LEGACY OF A COUNTRY PRIEST

I never learned his name. He was simply "the curé of Sère-Lanso." In the 1960s, over the course of several years, I visited him regularly and stayed at the rectory. But I never heard him addressed as anything other than "Monsieur le Curé" by his parishioners, and "the curé of Sère-Lanso" when others were talking about him.

In a way, that was appropriate: his function defined him. He had been born in this small village in the foothills of the Pyrenees about six miles from Lourdes. He had entered the White Fathers in his youth, contracted tuberculosis, and been sent back to his natal village to die. But that was more than fifty years before I met him. He was in his eighties at the time, but still going strong—small, chubby, partially bald, but full of energy.

What led me to him originally was that he was rumored to be one of the few people still alive who had known Charles de Foucauld (1858–1916). He received me very cordially. I think he was just happy to have a visitor. The Foucauld theme was quickly exhausted. When the curé was a novice at Maison Carrée, the motherhouse of the White Fathers in Algeria, Foucauld had come to make a retreat. The novices were instructed to respect his privacy. Before he departed, however, Foucauld mingled a bit with the novices but didn't say much of anything. That was that.

The curé had no housekeeper and did all his own cooking and cleaning. His staple diet was a kind of pudding he made once a week. It lasted him the entire week and he called it "apostolic cement." A band of chickens ran free throughout the rectory. These were his "novices." When I stayed with him, one or another of the novices would disappear and wind up on my plate.

In his younger days, he would ride on horseback to visit the farms scattered over the mountainside. Now he used a *deux chevaux* (a two-horsepower Citroën). Getting the car out of the garage was an adventure. There was a slope in front of the garage. The curé would put a wooden wedge on the slope, release the brake, let the car slide down until it hit the wedge, close the garage door, and get in the car. There was no margin for error, but somehow he managed to pull it off every time.

He would get up around 4 a.m. and go to his unheated church, where he would recite his breviary and pray in silence until dawn. But there was absolutely nothing pious or churchy about him. He talked about the things of God matter-of-factly, simply and naturally, as if this dimension of reality were obvious to everyone. He had a peasant's common sense, was a consummate storyteller, and had a great sense of humor. Once when I was visiting, he had to go for an interview with the bishop. When he returned, he told me that he had made a good impression, and that the bishop had found him younger in spirit than most of the priests in his diocese. He responded to the bishop, "But of course! I'm in my second childhood!"

Everyone in Sère-Lanso attended Mass on Sunday, and if they didn't, they'd better have a good excuse. It was obvious that they cherished this old man. There was no choir, but the curé had some chants on a tape recorder that he would start and stop during the liturgy, with varying success. I began going to Sère-Lanso whenever I had the chance. The peace, goodness, and detachment of Monsieur le Curé simplified my own life and dispelled all the false problems I was creating for myself. I had no doubt that I was in the presence of a saint.

For twenty years, the curé of Sère-Lanso had also been the diocesan exorcist for Lourdes. Out of the hundreds of cases that were presented to him, only two were serious enough to have necessitated an exorcism. The others, he said, were simply instances of mental illness. I can't recall the second case, but the first one kept me from sleeping the night he described it. It had to do with a nun from a convent in Montpellier.

She began having inexplicable seizures, especially after receiving Communion. She would spit out the host and blaspheme in a voice that was not her own. She was taken to a hospital and observed during one of these seizures. While it lasted, welts appeared on her body, only to disappear without leaving a trace once the seizure was over. This led the nun's community to bring her to Lourdes for an exorcism. The curé interviewed her and found her to be perfectly normal otherwise, and even a very holy person. But for the first time, he consented to do an exorcism.

It took place in a chapel of the basilica of Lourdes, which could be sealed off from the public. Two members of the nun's community accompanied her. There was a marble altar, and the curé stood behind it as he began the ritual. As soon as he started reciting the opening prayers, the nun stiffened ("like this fork," he said as he described the event) and flew up to the ceiling at the far end of the chapel. Then, in a guttural voice, she accused the curé of hypocrisy and began relating all his sins and failings. The curé, now totally terrified, crouched behind the altar and, at full speed, continued with the prayers of the ritual. Once he finished, the nun came swooping down and smashed headfirst into the altar. The curé was certain she had been killed and hesitated several seconds before venturing out from behind the altar to assess the situation. The nun was sitting there, dazed, but she had no physical injuries. Nor did she remember anything that had happened—she never did when she had these seizures. I asked the curé the obvious question: Did the exorcism work? He didn't know. He had never heard anything more about the nun.

In contrast to this dramatic incident, the curé encountered many other, if less troubling, phenomena in his visits to the outlying farms in the parish. Over the years, he was summoned because a family claimed an "evil eye" had been put on them. In these cases, the curé went directly inside to inspect the mattresses and pillows, which were often stuffed with eiderdown. If he found that the feathers were interwoven and impossible to pull apart, then he would have them burned. That usually sufficed to dissipate the curse. His explanation was that the whole region was at one time under the influence of a mysterious sect known as the Cathars. During the Middle Ages, they were widespread in Southern France. They left no written records and relied on oral traditions. The little we do know about them comes from the records of the Inquisition. They were essentially Manicheans who believed in a dual and conflictive principle of good and evil. Vestiges of their beliefs continued in the oral traditions and customs of the region.

But there was another manifestation he told me about. In his youth, the curé knew people who had been alive at the time of the apparitions at Lourdes. Their recollections centered on the visions but also on what happened in the surrounding area at the time. There had been a sort of collective hysteria, with children claiming to have experienced similar visions and displaying disturbing sorts of behavior. The curé understood all this to be a diabolical reaction to the apparitions themselves. Yet it was this sense of anarchy that remained engraved in the memory of many of the local population. What was a light for the rest of the world seemed to be a scandal and a cross for them.

In certain respects, the curé of Sère-Lanso and his rural parish were a throwback to the Middle Ages, to a sacral society where supernatural realities went unquestioned, and where angels and demons struggled for people's souls. We have come a long way from that world and have become much more sophisticated. But are we wiser? Is the perspective of the curé so naive and antiquated that it can be entirely explained away? Or does it have elements of truth that we may have neglected? St. Paul reminds us "our struggle is not with flesh and blood but with the principalities, with the powers of this dark world and with the spiritual forces of evil in the regions above" (Eph. 6:12).

The curé knew full well that the external manifestations of the powers of darkness are but signs of the deeper, ongoing mystery of evil, an evil far more subtle than the manifestations themselves. But while there is a danger of attaching exaggerated importance to the exterior signs, there is also the opposite risk of discounting them to the point we risk minimizing them and forgetting the mystery they signify. Science may explain—or try to explain—phenomena once regarded as supernatural. And no doubt some of these explanations prove valid on a strictly empirical level. But the question persists whether such explanations alone account for the profound, humanly haunting significance of some of these phenomena.

Further, exterior signs of evil and grace may have nothing to do with the goodness of the people involved. The victim of a diabolical possession is not made evil by it, any more than the recipient of a miracle is automatically "sanctified." In the case of the possessed nun, it might well be that she served as a providential manifestation of satanic power in order to remind us of its reality. In the Gospel accounts, Jesus himself is described as being physically transported by the Evil One to a high mountain to be tempted, and then to the pinnacle of the Temple. But these very encounters become the occasion for Jesus to manifest his obedience to the Father. For as real as the powers might be, in the last analysis their influence is limited and subject to the power of life itself. That is the message of the book of Revelation: despite all appearances, there is a final victory—one that assures us of God's confidence in us.

The curé of Sère-Lanso defied categorization. He was open-minded, interested in everything, curious about modern science, and sympathetic toward efforts to renew the church. His bishop was right: he was young in spirit, disposed to learn and to revise himself. Yet his feet were planted firmly on the ground and in the concrete reality of his little parish. He had experienced Satan and his works in all their crudity, named them, and taken their measure. The result was a palpable peace and an optimism that was rooted in deep humility. He was not one of the tormented priests of Bernanos, nor did he take himself all that seriously. What he did take seriously was the victory of Christ over the Prince of Darkness, which he experienced as an undeniable fact. And he lived in the simple radiance of that joy.

October 7, 2011

KNOWING JESUS

A while back, I was asked to write about "what the person of Jesus meant to me." I took this as a request to describe my personal relationship to Jesus. To my humiliation—and perhaps to my enlightenment—I realized that I didn't have a clue about how to answer this. Did I even have such a relationship? In faith, I believe that Jesus has a relationship to me—but is this reciprocal? And to what point? In the ordinary course of my days, my chief preoccupation is not to put on the mind of Christ, to refer everything to him as to one constantly accompanying me. My chief preoccupation is trying not to get hurt or bored too much in the give-and-take of daily life.

But there is another way of interpreting the question. It could mean: How do I see Jesus of Nazareth? I see Jesus as the church presents him to me, through Scripture and through the apostolic tradition as defined in the great councils—as true God and true man, one Person in two natures "without separation, without mixture, without confusion and without change." I take this teaching at its word, very literally. When we affirm that Jesus of Nazareth is true God of true God, that must be understood absolutely. When we affirm that Jesus is true man, that too must be understood absolutely. One of the Holy Trinity, who thundered on Mount Sinai and before whom the seraphim veil their faces, became an insignificant worker in an occupied and oppressed country, was dragged through the streets of Jerusalem as "an utter and ignominious failure" and put to death as a political agitator. Neither of these terms should be watered down even though, psychologically, we cannot conceive them simultaneously. Our faith does not ask us to try to reconcile these absolutes; it asks us to affirm them. Sometimes we will be struck more by the fact that Jesus is every bit as human as you or I; on other occasions it will be the fact that he is God. When we speak of the mystery of the Incarnation, we will necessarily emphasize one or the other of these terms. Any attempt to reconcile the two terms rationally would lead to a diminution of both. I don't think we should be afraid to follow these affirmations to their necessary consequences. This man who plunks himself down by a well in Samaria, tired, hungry, and thirsty, is the co-eternal Word through whom all things were made. When we affirm that Jesus is true man, I think this applies not only to his human nature but also to his human destiny. The adage of St. Athanasius that "what has not been assumed has not been redeemed," which became the rule of orthodoxy during the Christological disputes, tells us something about the way God is man. A human being evolves, learns, is shaped by his surroundings, fears and hesitates, has good days and bad—all this is part of being human, limited and vulnerable. Our God did not play at being man. The human nature that was integrated into the second person of the Trinity was not an abstract human nature; it was taken from the flesh of Mary of Nazareth in the days when Quirinius was governor of Syria. When we speak of the historical humanity of Jesus, then, we are concentrating on one aspect of a scandalous mystery. One of the Holy Trinity became, in all truth, our brother and "like us in every way except sin," and we affirm everything that this implies. Biblical criticism, rightly used, brings this reality into relief. In his *Introduction to New Testament Christology*, Raymond Brown concludes that there is no compelling evidence in the synoptic gospels that Jesus ever presented himself as God or had a clear vision of the redemptive nature of his passion and death. This became clear to the church only after Pentecost, and then little by little. Like the rest of us, Jesus had to learn obedience in a certain obscurity, truly resist the temptations that presented themselves throughout his whole life, discover his destiny progressively. Is this incompatible with his divine nature? Chalcedon says no—that God became true man. In this sense, no Christology can be too "low." Nor can there be a Christology that is too "high." This very tension is essential to the mystery.

The Congregation for the Doctrine of the Faith has insisted that Jesus of Nazareth had the "beatific vision." But this does not mean that the vision illuminated his consciousness in such a way that past, present, and future were all perfectly clear to him, or that he always understood his divine identity in all its aspects. Otherwise he would be like an actor merely playing the role of a man—an idea I find repugnant. So how did the beatific vision affect Jesus before his glorification? Perhaps we can imagine it along the lines of how sanctifying grace affects us: it guides us as a kind of instinct when we are faithful to it, and yet it remains beyond our conceptual grasp. Just as sanctifying grace is a participation in the divine life, the grace of the hypostatic union would have been experienced by Jesus as an eternal identity but also as a total poverty and dependence. Jesus, Word of God and son of Mary, would have been aware that he receives absolutely everything from the Father—that without the Father he is nothing—and he would have experienced this as no one else has. The cry of the abandoned Christ on the Cross is that of a divine and human dereliction beyond words, beyond imaginings.

Yet this historical Jesus who walked the streets of Nazareth and Capernaum, who suffered under Pontius Pilate and rose on the third day, is essentially a memory. His presence to me today is otherwise mysterious. His presence is as hidden as it was in Nazareth, where he was simply known as the carpenter, the son of Mary and brother to James and Joseph and Jude and Simon. He has promised to be with us until the end of the world, as he was present in the silence of Nazareth and in the silence of the Cross. His brothers and sisters and mothers will forever be those who, in the depths of their hearts, hear the word of God and keep it, whether they realize it or not. His presence is hidden in the Eucharist and in the people of good will who surround us and who, in the secret of their hearts, shelter Jesus and resemble him—as siblings resemble one another.

St. Gregory of Nyssa wrote: "Never think of the Son without thinking of the Spirit." The reverse would be equally true: Never think of the Spirit without thinking of the Son. For St. Irenaeus, the Son and the Spirit are "the two hands of the Father" that always work together. This is evident in the gospels. If it is Jesus who promises to send the Holy Spirit to accompany his disciples after his glorification, it is the Spirit who announced Jesus through the prophets; it is through the Spirit that he becomes incarnate in the womb of Mary, is manifested in the waters of the Jordan, is led into the desert, and is resurrected from the dead. In the Eucharist, it is the Spirit that transforms the gifts and is present in the body and blood of Christ consumed by the community. The Spirit reveals and sends Jesus, as Jesus reveals and sends the Spirit, and both reveal the Father. This is an aspect of the Trinity that has often been neglected in the Western Church. Without the Spirit the Word cannot be heard. Without the Word the Spirit is inarticulate.

In the book *Examining the Catholic Intellectual Tradition*, Robert Imbelli points out that, after a long period of Christo-monism in the church, there is now a sort of Holy Spirit–monism: a vague, generic "spirituality" that neglects Christ. Perhaps the relationship between Word and Spirit is somewhat analogous to the relationship between God and man in Christology. We have difficulty in imagining the two terms simultaneously and tend to oppose them, whereas they are always both present and active together. We oppose the "institutional church," structured by the Word, to the "prophetic church" structured by the Spirit. But the institutional church should itself be prophetic, the Word leading to the Spirit and the Spirit to the Word. Obviously, this has not always been the case in the church's history—and it will never be entirely the case until the consummation of the Kingdom—but this is the eschatological reality toward which we tend and for which we hope.

Still, when I look at the historical Jesus and the mystery of the church, I'm looking at things from the outside, as it were, seeing them as objects. I can be in awe of these mysteries and the quality of love they manifest, just as I have been in awe of the Alhambra of Grenada, the Cathedral of Chartres, or the Winged Victory of Samothrace, where one passes from simple beauty to irresistible magic. Such an appreciation is, I believe, very good and a kind of grace. By itself, however, it does not put me in contact with the person of Jesus, the Word made flesh, the Life of the world, and the Life of my life. It can remain at the level of a consoling, edifying, and elevating poetic intuition.

True experimental knowledge of Jesus comes only through the Holy Spirit, and it does not come easily. What makes it hard is not any lack of generosity on the part of God but our own opacity. In an article in the February 27, 2004 *Commonweal*, Rachelle Linner cited a passage from Flannery O'Connor that immediately resonated in me: "Human nature is so faulty that it can resist any amount of grace and most of the time it does." Most of the time, I am much more aware of this resistance than of whatever might somehow get past it.

There are those who speak of the encounter with the person of Jesus as a pivotal, decisive experience. Such an experience might, indeed, be valid for some. Its authenticity will manifest itself by its fruits. Kierkegaard, on another level, speaks of a decisive act of commitment—and we are constantly summoned to "conversion," to repent and change. Classical theology has the angels deciding their destiny in a single, unalterable choice. I sometimes dream of being able to imitate such an act, one that would free me from all my ambiguities and contradictions, my half-hearted aspirations and ineffectual resolutions. This is not the way things work, however. For us, the life of faith is not an instantaneous, once-and-for-all decision, but a long series of decisions, a pilgrimage that, like any other journey, includes its share of tedium, confusion, and risk. So my relationship to the living Christ and the life-giving Spirit remains a mystery to me. I entrust myself into the hands of a God who is greatly merciful and knows out of what clay he has fashioned us. He has also said, "He who comes to me, I will not cast out." I take him at his word.

May 15, 2015

C hristian mysticism can be defined as the experience of direct, personal encounter with the God of love. It is an immediate experience, one that transcends all rituals and dogmas. It goes deeper than all "signs," whether verbal or sacramental, to attain what they only hint at or point toward. Christian mysticism requires purification, a heightening of the senses and of the spirit. It is not the fruit of abstract reflection or of intellectual intuition. It is a gift of God, but one often associated with the practice of contemplative prayer.

Over centuries of Christian history, such experiences of God increasingly became the domain of a small elite. Mystics' lives were consecrated to the pursuit of holiness and to preparing themselves for the reception of this gift. Such a vocation was itself considered a "state of perfection." The earliest mystics of the church were the desert fathers and mothers. In later Western Christianity, this role was assumed by contemplative communities like the Carmelites, Carthusians, and Trappists, but there remained individual, if sometimes idiosyncratic, "fools for Christ." Gradually there developed classical texts, designed to guide souls in their experience of God. These included *The Ladder of Perfection* of St. John Climacus (c. 569–c. 649), *The Ascent of Mount Carmel* of St. John of the Cross (1542–91), and *The Interior Castle* of St. Teresa of Ávila (1515–82).

Implicit in these approaches was the assumption that mystical union with God is a life-consuming task, one that requires separation from the world with all its temptations and distractions (one of the themes of Thomas Merton's 1948 bestseller *The Seven Storey Mountain*). In this tradition, the mystical experience was reserved to those who mastered certain techniques, who had the leisure to pursue such a quest, and who experienced the "mystical states" described in the manuals. But such an approach carried with it an inherent danger: the goal could devolve into seeking one's own personal peace and perfection. Further, an introverted form of contemplation, coupled with rigid asceticism, could result in a tendency to regard God as a mental object, which in turn could lead some to think that "love of God alone" must exclude all other objects.

Ironically, it was a cloistered Carmelite nun who dynamited these assumptions. St. Thérèse of Lisieux (1873–97), with her "little way," opened the possibility of a contemplative life for all, one that looked on the world not with disgust but with compassion. She saw her vocation as being "love in the heart of the church," and this did not entail flight from the world but a remarkable attention to its salvation. For this young nun, her call was not to be a solitary contemplative but an active member of the Mystical Body. And to do this she had to be acutely concerned with the fate of all. This dimension had never been absent from the church's mystics, but Thérèse made it explicit.

Less than twenty years after her death, Jacques (1882–1973) and Raïssa Maritain (1883–1960) would take things further still. As active laypeople in the world who possessed a deep desire to know and love God, the Maritains emphasized the elements of a lay spirituality they found in the Thomistic tradition. It defined the contemplative life as one rich in the gifts of the Holy Spirit. These gifts, imparted to all believers at baptism and confirmation, were meant to govern all aspects of their lives. One or another (or several) of them might predominate in a person's life, depending on temperament or concrete circumstances. And some are exceedingly practical: prudence, justice, fortitude, and temperance, for example. But the Maritains also postulated, rather timidly, a grace of "nontypical" or "masked" contemplation for those unable to achieve the dispositions necessary for the classical contemplative life pursued in the monastic orders. A contemplative life amid the noise, rush, and ambiguities of the world will be vastly different from the well-ordered life of the monk or contemplative nun. This recognition marked a further step in articulating the contemplative life "in the world" and linking it to the baptismal grace every Christian receives. This sort of new awareness continued to develop in the years preceding Vatican II.

But the world also changed. The essentially rural, sacral society of the Middle Ages was dislodged by the industrial revolution and the emergence of the secular nation-state. And the evolution of technology was even more dramatic: from quills and carriages to computers and space travel. Those of us living in today's world of twenty-four-hour news cycles, global financial markets, and personal iPods are exposed to an onrush of information and distraction that is the antithesis of traditional contemplative silence. Moreover, because of technology, work itself is becoming more rushed, competitive, and demanding.

The documents of Vatican II reaffirmed the baptismal dignity of the people of God as kings, prophets, and priests. Laypeople were no longer to be considered simply obedient, submissive sheep, but were called to be active participants in the life of the church and the world. Henceforth it would be impossible to exclude them from full participation in the church's life, including its contemplative dimension.

Since the council there has been a flourishing of retreats and institutes, prayer and study groups, lay affiliations with the traditional monastic orders. This is, in itself, a very positive development, but it is not something everyone can get involved in. It takes time and even money to make a retreat, and not everyone functions well in group settings or has the intellectual and religious background for this sort of practice. I sometimes wonder whether our conception of "lay spirituality" is not itself elitist—in the sense that it is generally defined by the more articulate, materially comfortable, and better educated members of the lay community. This is, perhaps, inevitable, but the preoccupations and sensitivities of this group are not necessarily those of others in the pews. If the "laity" is to be heard, the quieter, more discreet voices of the "faceless" ones must be sought out and taken into consideration.

Of course, there are other types of mysticism that are not specifically Christian. There is what Jacques Maritain called "natural mysticism," a state that can be reached by diligent human effort. Through physical asceticism and mental concentration, a person can arrive at an intuition of God's creative act that starts and sustains everything in existence. This can be an exhilarating experience— perhaps the summit of what a person can achieve through his or her effort. But this is not what Christians understand as the experience of

God's inner mystery. Such an experience can coexist with authentic Christian mysticism, but the two operate on different planes. For "natural mysticism" does not involve salvific knowledge. Still, as a gift of God founded on love, Christian mysticism is not limited to members of the church alone, even as the church and its teachings point the way and dispose us toward reception of this salvific gift. These in turn situate, articulate, and sustain its reception. But there remain no limits to God's generosity, mercy, and self-revelation.

Vatican II ratified this understanding when it looked beyond the visible frontiers of the church to recognize the workings of the Holy Spirit in other religions and in all people of goodwill, all images of the living God. As Jesus taught, every act of authentic goodness comes from the Father of Lights. Swiss Cardinal Charles Journet (1891–1975), who attended the council, had a very simple and luminous formula: Whatever is pure, in any of us, belongs to the church. The church visible should be a sacrament of grace and mercy that extends beyond itself and embraces all human beings. But the institutional church is only the tip of the iceberg. Through it the kingdom is manifest visibly on earth, illumined by faith and fortified by the sacraments. But the church itself journeys in a more hidden manner, in the pure and loving hearts of all peoples, and it reaches its goal through the mystery of the Cross.

I have a number of co-workers who are immigrants. They work two or more jobs, not to purchase luxuries, but to survive and to give their kids a decent education, as well as to help family members in their country of origin. What type of "prayer life" can they have? Gandhi once said that courage is the treasure of the poor. Would not the fortitude of these individuals, who sacrifice themselves through love and without reserve or afterthought, be a gift from the Holy Spirit—a means in itself of "knowing God"? Not conceptually but by "connaturality"—for God, in the Trinitarian mystery, is pure gift. Might not this be the genuine "prayer of the poor" that God hears? There is a saying of the desert fathers that has lost none of its edge: "Shed your blood and receive the Holy Spirit." It is in the gift of self that a person becomes more and more an image of the living

God, revealing the Father manifested by the Son and the Holy Spirit. As St. Augustine says in *De Trinitate*, "If you see love, you see the Trinity." God's love is revealed as both crucified and beatific, as all-embracing and yet unutterable.

St. Augustine also has this wonderful passage: "Love is a powerful thing, my brothers and sisters. Do you wish to see how powerful love is? Whoever, through some necessity, cannot accomplish what God commands, let him love the one who accomplishes it and thus he accomplishes it in that other." According to Journet's formula, whatever is done in goodness belongs to the church and is "assumed" in its intentions, incorporated into its collective prayer and the life of the communion of the saints.

Today, the purifications described by the classical spiritual masters are brought about through the suffering of the poor—what they endure through the events of their lives and at the hands of others. Their sufferings are often shouldered without the self-pity characteristic of more "sensitive" souls. The fruit of all this is lives of palpable simplicity and a genuine sense of peace. It is not, however, simply a stoic acceptance of destiny but an authentic love for others that includes a hunger and a thirst for justice, even when events make one feel powerless. A true contemplative life, then, includes a social dimension, a desire to wipe away the tears of others. Such a vision instinctively longs to sees others as God sees them, in their grandeur and dignity, and to experience their defilement as insupportable and blasphemous. The fact that Christ remains crucified in these little ones, that he suffers with them and refuses to descend from his cross, remains a scandal. At the same time, it confirms an obstinate hope and a sense of promise. This is what distinguishes Christian mysticism from gnosticism, certain Asian spiritualities, and other forms of contemporary "spirituality."

One of my workmates is a mechanic. I've known him for more than a decade. We pull one another's leg a lot. He bums tobacco from me (we both roll our own), and he's a bit of a character—especially when he's had a few beers. But it was only recently that I learned, through a newspaper article, that he and his wife had taken in an incredible number of foster children over the years. When I asked him about it, he told me quite simply of the multiple joys and sorrows this had brought him. His obvious love for these children whom nobody wanted, his generosity and willingness to accept heartbreak, was so far beyond anything I was capable of that I could only admire it from a distance. The guy is not particularly pious or intellectual. He simply gives, without fanfare and without expecting anything in return.

In his autobiographical short story "The House of Matryona," Aleksandr Solzhenitsyn describes a poor woman whose life has been a series of disappointments and humiliations, but who obstinately, even foolishly, continues to help others. After her death in a tragic accident, the narrator concludes: "We had lived side by side with her and had never understood that she was the righteous one without whom— as the proverb says—no village can stand. Nor any city. Nor our whole land." I am no Medjugorje enthusiast, but I was struck by the response that the Virgin purportedly gave to one of the visionaries, when asked who was the holiest person in the village. It turned out to be an old Muslim woman no one had paid much attention to.

Although the baptized have been given grace and enlightenment, this turns out to be more a responsibility than a privilege. It has to be responded to and interiorized. Nor are Christians automatically better than others. Far from it. Of those to whom much is given, much is required. Like the visible church, contemplative orders are signs of the kingdom to come. That some of the baptized are able to dedicate themselves entirely to developing an awareness of the presence of God bears testimony to the church's eschatological hope and understanding. But when all is said and done, we have no idea of who carries whom in the great mystery of the communion of the saints. That fact should be a source of both hope and humility.

The mystical life of the church is part of its essence. In its profound silence, hidden in the depths of hearts, it is known only to God. It is a gift, as God is Gift, in the Trinitarian mystery and in the redemptive Incarnation.

December 17, 2010

A FAITH FOR FAILURES

I first learned of Shusaku Endo's 1969 historical novel *Silence* years ago in *Commonweal*. In 2016, Martin Scorsese adapted the book into a feature film.

Silence tells the story of a Jesuit priest, Fr. Rodrigues, who sets out for Japan during a furious persecution of the Christian community there. His mission is to minister to the surviving Christians and to find out what has happened to the Jesuit provincial, who has dropped out of sight. A few months after arriving, Rodrigues is taken prisoner. From his squalid cell, he can see Japanese Christians suspended by rope over a dung pile and slowly bleeding to death. They have already apostatized. If Rodrigues will apostatize too, they will be released and treated. If not, they will die a slow and terrible death.

Faced with this dilemma, the Jesuit receives a visit from Fr. Ferreira, the missing provincial. Ferreira, it turns out, has chosen apostasy, and tries to persuade Rodrigues to do the same. The act of apostasy consists in trampling on an image of Christ. In response to the stubborn resistance of his former student, Ferreira accuses Rodrigues of weakness. He says Rodrigues's fear of betraying Christ and the church is really a fear of betraying his own self-image. Ferreira claims that Christ himself would have apostatized to save these Christians from their torment and pleads with Rodrigues to "perform the most painful act of love that has ever been performed." Rodrigues finally gives in, and, as he raises his foot, the image of Christ he's about to step on speaks to him: "Trample! Trample! I more than anyone know of the pain in your foot. Trample! It was to be trampled upon by men that I was born into the world. It was to share men's pain that I carried my cross!" The book has a depressing ending. Ferreira and Rodriguez, known derisively as Peter and Paul, spend the rest of their lives under house arrest. They are provided with Japanese wives and live in relative comfort, without too much to do. Fr. Rodrigues is commissioned to write a disavowal of his faith and does so. Father Ferriera has already written his. They cannot stand one another because each reminds the other of himself.

When I finally got around to reading *Silence*, I came down with a severe and demoralizing case of pneumonia that had me hospitalized for two weeks. Endo's book, based on a true story, did not exactly boost my morale. But I think it touches on a very profound truth about God: his voluntary powerlessness.

Christ, the Suffering Servant, descended into hell to raise the dead and to found a new order of things, where the last shall be first and the first last. In a review for *Commonweal* of a book on St. Augustine ("Choosing the Better Part," June 17, 2017), James Wetsel attributes the saint's conversion to his discovery of the humility of God. It was this that also inspired Charles de Foucauld and Léon Bloy, who wrote, "God seems to have condemned himself until the end of time not to exercise any immediate right of a master over a servant or a king over a subject. We can do what we want. He will defend himself only by his patience and beauty." The All-Powerful has become the very least, offering himself to be mocked and abused. We have, it is true, the promise of the eternal kingdom, but this is another order of reality, one we can hope for but not imagine. What we experience on this side of death is the scandalizing powerlessness of God.

There is another character who comes and goes throughout *Silence*, the apostate Kichijiro, who is a sort of Judas figure. It is he who first puts Fr. Rodrigues in contact with a community of Japanese Christians, and it is he who eventually betrays him. Yet Kichijiro is forever seeking forgiveness and absolution. He knows himself to be weak. If he had died ten years earlier, before the persecution of the Christians, he would have gone to Paradise a good and respected Christian. But now all is lost: the police use him and despise him. He despises himself. Yet hadn't Judas been a friend of Jesus, and surely Jesus prayed for him and loved him. At the moment of Judas's betrayal, Jesus spoke these sad and mysterious words: "Friend, do what you are here for!" For his part, Fr. Rodrigues gives Kichijiro absolution but cannot forgive him.

Reading *Silence* shook me up and left me with uncomfortable questions. How deep is my faith? Am I any better than Kichijiro—fine as long as it's easy to keep up appearances but not when I'm put to the test? Endo was once asked why he was so intrigued by apostates and other moral failures. His answer was that we can feel closer to them than to the heroic martyrs who held up under torture. I think that there is a great deal of truth in that. The church itself is built on the testimony of a betrayer and a coward, the great friend of Jesus who denied him three times. John the Baptist himself had doubts, sending his disciples to ask Jesus if he was really the messiah. Like Christ himself, many of the saints were tempted to abandon their mission, and some of them yielded to the temptation, but they did not yield to despair. Having fallen, they rose again.

January 6, 2017

THE OTHER GUY

When I was a boy the third person of the Trinity was referred to as the Holy Ghost. I recall not being too keen on doing business with a ghost, however holy he might be. It is now more usual to speak of the "Holy Spirit." Perhaps this makes him less intimidating for little kids, yet for most of us he is still the "other guy"—a sort of phantom shrouded in mystery.

In the psychology of the Western church, the main drama of salvation is played out between the Father and the Son. It is only at Pentecost, when all has been accomplished, that the Paraclete promised by Jesus enters the scene. The Holy Spirit is presented as depending on the Word for its temporal manifestation as well as its eternal procession. This, in turn, leads us to consider the church as primarily the church of the Incarnate Word—rationally structured, ordered, determined in its intelligibility—and only secondarily "pneumatic." The Holy Spirit seems almost like an afterthought. In *Papal Sins*, Garry Wills claims that many of the prerogatives of the Holy Spirit have gradually been transferred to the Virgin Mary—as if an embodied person, one of us, had to replace the Holy Spirit in the role of comforter.

In short, there is a certain malaise in the Catholic Church when it comes to the Holy Spirit. We do not quite know what to say about this nebulous and somewhat isolated presence. It is significant that, at Vatican II, it was the Orthodox observers who pointed out to the council fathers the lack of references to the Holy Spirit in their proposed texts. The texts were revised, but the malaise remains.

The intuitions of the Eastern Churches might be of help to us. "Never think of the Son without thinking of the Holy Spirit," wrote St. Gregory of Nyssa. St. Irenaeus speaks of the Son and the Spirit as the "two hands of the Father," and the Father always uses both hands at the same time. The Word and the Spirit work together from the very beginning. If it is the Son who gives the Spirit; it is the Spirit who reveals and makes present the Son. At the origin of all things, it is the Spirit who hovers over the primal waters preparing them to receive the creative Word. It is the Spirit who inspires the prophets of Israel and prepares the revelation of the Logos made flesh. It is by the Spirit's power that the Virgin Mary conceives Emmanuel and God dwells among us. It is the Spirit who manifests Jesus in the waters of the Jordan and leads him into the desert. Throughout his life, Jesus is obedient to the Spirit of his Father. His final act will be the remission of the Spirit to the Father—so that Christ, "abandoned," might enter into the silence and solitude of the tomb and of hell, and thus shatter the bonds of death. The Spirit will seal this triumph and raise him up on the third day. Finally, it is through the Spirit that the grace of the risen Christ is poured forth on his church.

It is also the Spirit who transforms the gifts into the Body and Blood of Christ in the Eucharist. When we receive Christ in the Eucharist, we also receive the Holy Spirit. It is the function of the Holy Spirit to make the presence of Christ a vivifying and permanent reality in the church, transforming a community of sinners into the Body of Christ. The Gospel message is not credible—not for others and not for us—unless the Paraclete has first prepared the mind and the heart to receive it. And when, in the silence of our innermost being, we listen to the voice of prayer springing up in our heart, it is not our own voice we hear but that of the Spirit speaking within us, revealing the Father and the Son.

In the Eastern tradition, the Son reveals and sends the Spirit as the Spirit reveals and sends the Son, and both proceed from the Father. Without the Spirit, the Word is mute; without the Word, the Spirit is inarticulate. Both are needed to manifest the Father of Lights. The return to such a tradition in the West might enable us to recover a sense of intimacy with the mysterious Third Person, who is too often discussed impersonally, as if he were just a theological abstraction.

This intimacy would not evacuate the mystery. The Spirit remains discreet and veiled. He is not in the earthquake or hurricane but reveals himself in the light breeze. He is flame, unction, perfume, a dove—insinuating himself in the ordinary. His *kenosis*, or self-emptying, parallels that of the Son. He is the Father of the poor

(*Veni pater pauperum*) who makes known the presence of Jesus in every person but especially in the powerless, the weak, the helpless. The very nature of his revelation is self-effacement. Yet outside of him there is no truth.

July 7, 2017

WHY I STAY CATHOLIC

Some time back, I got an e-mail from an old friend with whom I had lost contact many years before. He was an ex-seminarian from Argentina who had been imprisoned and tortured during the "dirty war" of the military dictatorship. That he had gotten out alive bordered on the miraculous.

His scars were real and permanent. Not the least of them were psychological wounds caused by the silence of most of the Argentine hierarchy and the active collaboration of some of its members during that period of brutal repression. So I was not overly surprised when he told me he had left the Catholic Church. His faith was intact, but he had lost all confidence in the institution. Initially, he found a home in the Episcopal Church, but there was no Episcopalian community where he was now living. He had also been attracted to the spirituality of Orthodoxy, but there was no Orthodox church near him. So he was praying alone with icons—as if it were only in the church triumphant, free of all ambiguity, that he could find his community. He could do much worse. He sent me a long list of grievances against the Catholic Church—most of which are very well founded. Far be it from me to judge my friend. I understand him all too well. He made me question my own motives for remaining in the church.

The most obvious and simple reason is that I'm used to it. I was born and brought up Catholic. I happen to be Catholic just as I happen to be American. It's an empirical fact—the rather prosaic underpinning of my fidelity.

Because I'm a Catholic, I go to Mass on Sundays (or Saturday evening), and I'm relatively at ease. I know when to sit, stand, and kneel, and I know the responses. I am deeply aware of Eucharistic theology, and I want to respond to this gift with all my being. Yet I often feel as though I'm just going through the motions. The people around me are strangers, the music is led by a choir singing a couple of octaves above what most of us are capable of, the songs themselves are sickly sentimental, and the sermon is often insipid. It has occurred to me that I feel more "at one" with the people on the 5 a.m. bus I take to work every morning than with the people at church. We at least know one another, however superficially, and we are on a similar adventure. At church, I have the impression that we are a motley crew fulfilling an obligation. There is a clique of dedicated people in the parish who keep things rolling, but I've never been tempted to become part of that group. I simply don't have a vocation to lay ministry. These are very good people who are trying their best. The worst of it is that I haven't a clue as to how things could be improved.

So I can't stand outside and throw stones. The very things that pain and disappoint me in the church exist in myself, and I don't like them there either. Often I feel like a hypocrite among hypocrites—all of us pretending to live something we are constantly contradicting.

That is the nitty-gritty level. In the larger context, there is a whole litany of complaints: the church's obsession with micromanaging the sexual life of the faithful and imposing its one-size-fits-all regulations; its courtship of the rich and powerful (who are the laypeople who sit on diocesan boards and consulting committees? Are they representative of the people of God?); the political posturing (morality must be legislated). The litany could go on and on.

Along with being a practicing Catholic, for the past fifteen years I have been singing in the choir of a small Russian Orthodox community. Through this I have discovered the riches of the Eastern churches, and this, in turn, has opened my eyes to aspects of my own tradition I hadn't seen before. This has been a wonderful, vivifying gift, but I have never been tempted to convert to Orthodoxy and am excluded from its sacraments. The contradictions in Orthodoxy are perhaps very different from those in Catholicism, but they are no less real. There is nothing "mystical" about the interchurch squabbles, the jurisdictional rivalries, and the petty jealousies. I've often felt that if the purest part of each tradition were to complement that of the other, many of the shortcomings of both would disappear.

But this would require a purification and an openness neither side seems willing to assume.

Is it simply out of inertia that I continue to be a Catholic? I hope not. Faced with so much that puts me off and the temptation to simply walk away, I find myself replying with Peter: "To whom else will we go? You have the words of eternal life."

A long time ago I copied a phrase from a now-forgotten source that goes to the heart of the matter: "We know what is human in the church...in the measure in which we are unworthy of knowing what is divine in it. Those who are best qualified for taking scandal at the faults, defects, and even deformities in the church—the saints—are those who never complain about them." Not being a saint, I complain, as at least some of them surely did. Still, I want to know and to believe in what is divine.

Our human communities will always be terribly imperfect, fragile, and ambiguous—sources of enriching friendships but also sources of antipathy and deception. The true Christian community is on a transcendental level, anchored in the Beatific Trinity, and hidden from human eyes. It is a communion of broken people who are very different from one another, who have different preoccupations and outlooks, but who nonetheless are united in the blood of Christ. I don't think we should pretend to "like" everyone, even if each is a good Catholic. The Apostles continued to bicker among themselves even after Pentecost. The history of the church is full of stories about saints who couldn't get along with one another. The failure of communion on a human level is part of our historicity and our legacy of sin. It is real and besets us from all sides. Yet this is precisely the raw material that becomes the temple of the Spirit and the body of Christ.

There is another aspect that is seldom mentioned: the very personal nature of our faith. What unites us, empirically, as Catholics is the profession of belief in the dogmas and teachings of the church. But the faith of each person is unique. If a hundred Catholics were asked what their faith means to them, there would be a hundred different answers. Faith is not simple acquiescence to an abstract dogma or teaching. It is an experience of Christ that leads one to make this dogma or teaching one's own, to appropriate it personally. It is not something that can be imposed, however subtly, from without. It must be vital and free, something understood and interpreted in the depths of one's being according to the gifts with which one has been graced, according to one's vocation and limitations. A faith that is not rooted in a deep interior conviction is not a living faith. We may not "feel" what we want to believe; we may even have surface doubts; but there is a core conviction that gives meaning to our existence, without which all would become an obscene joke. As a Catholic, my conviction is the love story the church offers me—the love of a God who becomes my brother, who suffers in me and with me, who takes upon himself the sin of the world, and descends to the depths of hell to seek what is lost. Although this gives meaning to my existence, it does not necessarily make me "feel good," for it challenges me at a level where I do not want to be challenged, and exacts more than I am comfortable giving. What the church puts before me is the wisdom of centuries: of confessors and martyrs and fools for Christ. This wisdom is incarnate in the ambiguities of both history and my own life, but it represents the continuity of the communion of the saints, the heritage bequeathed to me by my ancestors in the faith.

In our better moments, when we have experienced what is divine in the church—and this requires discernment—the human element becomes less troubling. Then one experiences an obscure but real anchor, an instinct, I suppose, that is akin to the idea of the *sensus fidelium*.

Although faith is personal and individuated, it is not individualistic. On the contrary, none of us is saved or perishes alone. Our moral acts affect the whole body of Christ, for better or for worse. They know no limit of time or place. If there are many mansions in the house of the Father, I doubt any of them is single-occupancy. In spite of all the difficulties I experience being "at home" in collective worship or prayer groups, I have been terribly blessed with many profound and wonderful friendships. Even though the faith of each person is unique, there are affinities in grace—a certain common way of seeing things, of acting and reacting. Perhaps my deepest joy and surest support is this sense of sharing such affinities with others. It is as if we spontaneously recognize one another. There is no need for preliminaries; we are on the same wavelength, we understand one another, we feed off one another. I have experienced this both inside and outside the canonical boundaries of the Catholic Church. In one of her letters to Fr. Joseph Perrin, Simone Weil wrote: "Nothing among human things has such power to keep our gaze fixed ever more intensely upon God than friendship for the friends of God." For me, it is like a foretaste of the definitive Kingdom.

In a way, my "community" resembles that of my Argentine friend. It is composed of living icons—some of whom still walk this earth, others who, although deceased, live in God—a cloud of witnesses who sustain and encourage me and whose destiny is mysteriously linked to mine. I believe that we do something wonderful together, although I'm not exactly sure what that is—nor is it my business to know.

February 23, 2007

Renewal
and Realities

A GOD WHO TREMBLES

B enedict XVI's 2007 encyclical *Spe salvi* is magnificent as a theological lesson on the virtue of hope, drawing on Scripture and the church fathers to challenge the misplaced hopes of the modern world.

Nearly a century prior to Benedict's letter, Charles Péguy (1873–1914) published *The Porch of the Mystery of the Second Virtue*—also a meditation on hope, but this one by a poet and unlikely mystic in the middle of a harrowing personal drama. Where Benedict speaks to the intellect, Péguy speaks to the heart; where Benedict strives for clarity, Péguy hints at mystery, and does so with an irresistible tenderness.

Charles Péguy was born in Orleans, the son of a carpenter. His father was killed in the Franco-Prussian War when Charles was ten months old. His mother supported herself and her child by mending chairs. Charles received the customary religious education, made his first Communion, and excelled in his studies. In 1895, he enthusiastically "converted" to socialism and became a militant atheist. In 1897, he married Charlotte Baudouin, the sister of a close friend who had died prematurely. With her dowry, Péguy founded a socialist publishing house. While still believing firmly in the socialist ideal, Péguy became disillusioned with socialist politics and its compromises—especially during the Dreyfus Affair. When he lost control of the publishing house, through what might be called a "hostile takeover," he founded a journal called *Les Cahiers de la Quinzaine*, in which he could express himself more freely. That put him in a political no man's land. He was considered a traitor by the Left for his refusal to toe the party line, while the Right wanted nothing to do with him because of his socialist ideals. Both considered him an enemy. This ideological isolation continued throughout his lifetime and followed him after his death.

In 1908, after a serious illness and a period of extreme distress, Péguy returned to Catholicism. His was the church of Joan of Arc and the cathedral-builders, of a time when France was the church's beloved elder daughter, pure and firm in its faith, when society lived according to the pulse of the liturgy, when God was quite naturally everywhere and in all things. Peguy's conversion was absolute and all-absorbing, as is evident in his postconversion writings. Yet he had not been married in the church, and his wife wanted no part of it—nor would she tolerate the idea of baptizing their three children. Charles Péguy thus found himself a "public sinner" in the church he so loved, cut off from the Eucharist and the rest of the sacraments. Moreover, he had fallen in love with Blanche Raphael, one of his associates at the *Cahiers*, and that passion was a further humiliation and contradiction, though Péguy successfully resisted the temptation and maintained his fidelity to his family. Raïssa Maritain describes Péguy praying with tears on the tops of omnibuses, entrusting his family to the Virgin. (After his death, his wife and children converted.) It was in the context of this personal anguish that he wrote his astonishing hymn to hope, *The Mystery of the Porch of the Second Virtue*. As a lieutenant in the army reserves, Péguy was mobilized at the outbreak of World War I. He was killed by a single bullet to the head in the Battle of the Marne.

Péguy's style is simple, lapidary, and, in some ways, biblical. Like the psalmists, he proceeds slowly, using rhythmic repetitions and slight variations to examine a theme in all its implications. It is contemplative poetry at its best, provoking prayer because it is imbued with prayer. Peter Maurin's prose style, in his *Easy Essays*, has often been compared to that of Péguy—though Maurin always denied that Péguy had any influence on him. Some of Péguy's works were translated into English in the 1940s, many of them by Julian Green, but translations are now difficult to find.

The Porch of the Mystery of the Second Virtue is the second part of a trilogy, sandwiched between *The Mystery of the Charity of Joan of Arc* and *The Mystery of the Holy Innocents*. All three are long poems in the form of dramatic plays. *The Mystery of the Charity of Joan of Arc* takes place before Joan is visited by her "voices." The dialogue involves three characters: Joan herself, who represents prophetic wisdom and impatience; Hauviette, a slightly older fellow shepherdess, who represents the wisdom of the world; and Madame Gervaise, a twenty-five-year-old Franciscan nun, who represents the wisdom of the church. The poem is a long meditation on the mystery of suffering. In one very poignant passage that has always haunted me, Hauviette discovers that Joan has nothing to eat for lunch. When pressed, Joan confesses that she had given the lunch her mother had prepared for her to two passing children who were fleeing the English invaders. The children had lost their parents and everything else; they did not know where they were going, and they were hungry. Hauviette reproaches Joan bitterly. What has she accomplished? The children will continue their aimless journey and will soon be hungry again, and now Joan, too, will be hungry. So three people will be hungry instead of two. According to Hauviette, Joan only makes herself suffer more by worrying about the children. Their misery reminds her of all who are hungry and miserable, of all who are neither fed nor consoled, and of those who no longer *want* to be consoled and despair of God's goodness. She makes herself suffer more than those who suffer these things. Joan can only repeat, "But they were hungry and were crying." Madame Gervaise offers the classical explanations but doesn't really solve the dilemma, or satisfy Joan. She speaks of the Passion of Christ and the sufferings of his mother.

In *The Porch of the Mystery of the Second Virtue*, Madame Gervaise, the sole protagonist, returns and addresses herself again to Joan. The anguished tone of *The Mystery of the Charity of Joan of Arc* has been replaced by a divine serenity. Madame Gervaise speaks in the name of God from the opening line: "The Faith that I like best, says God, is Hope." Hope is a little girl, apparently insignificant, who constantly astonishes God. Faith and charity one can understand. How can anyone who has seen the wonders of nature not believe? And charity is almost natural: to be distressed by the sufferings of others is part of our makeup. But hope is unexplainable. How can anyone, seeing how things have gone today (and the day before and the day before that) still go to bed thinking that all will be different tomorrow? Hope is God's greatest miracle; it astonishes even him.

Faith sees things as they are, charity loves things as they are, but hope sees and loves what *will* be.

Most Christians pay a lot of attention to faith and to charity. They are like hope's two elder sisters, the practical ones who have business to attend to, who seem to be dragging their insouciant little sister along. Hope's focus is elsewhere, but in reality it is she who is dragging her sisters along, for without her they would be nothing but a couple of old women going nowhere. Like a child, hope runs back and forth along the road, always going to the same place and making her sisters follow her. One would think that all the days and all the roads are the same, that the tracks of yesterday are erased by those of today and those of today by those of tomorrow. But for hope, every day is really a new adventure, the road is always new. The footprints are not effaced but put end to end, and they lead to eternity.

In one of his more audacious moves, Péguy attributes hope to God himself. "All the sentiments, all the movements we should have for God, God had them first for us." Not only did God love us first, before we loved him. He hoped in us first, so that we might hope in him. He had confidence in us, so that we might have confidence in him. Madame Gervaise, addressing herself to Joan the shepherdess, naturally invokes the parable of the Good Shepherd. There will be more joy in heaven for the one lost sheep than for the ninety-nine that were not lost—for these remained in faith and love. But the lost sheep caused God to be afraid and awoke hope in the heart of Jesus, the heart of God himself. God was afraid that this sheep might be definitively lost, and this fear made his love tremble. God was afraid that he might have to condemn this strayed one. Thus it was that the heart of Jesus and the heart of God trembled with fear and hope. And when the lost sheep was found, God, like the father of the prodigal son, experienced a new sentiment, a joy, a renewal, "as though he were a new God, eternally new." God has made himself dependent on the most miserable sinner because he hopes in him. He has put himself into the hands of the worst of us. He is afraid of the sinner because he is afraid *for* the sinner.

This brings us back to our hope in God. He who hopes in God is made pure, however soiled he may have been before. The miracle of hope makes clean the impure water; it is the fountain of youth and rebirth. It is easy enough to draw pure water from pure sources, but hope draws pure water from contaminated sources. Péguy certainly considered himself impure. All he dared ask of Our Lady of Chartres was "the last place in Purgatory."

The final pages of *The Porch of the Second Virtue* are dedicated to night—the time when men cease to act and God works in peace. Night is given to us so that we might abandon ourselves to God. Finally, the poem narrows this theme down to one particular night, the night of Good Friday, when darkness descends. Here Péguy opens the way toward a total theology of hope. He dares to speak in the name of God. He contemplates God's work in the hearts of men and women.

One of the most striking features of Péguy's religious poetry is that he never calls attention to himself; in fact, there is a complete and eloquent self-effacement. His entire focus is on God and his creation—and Péguy's God is very convincing. He knows very well of what clay he made us, yet that doesn't prevent him from sometimes being very surprised by what we can do with our gift of liberty, both in the way of holiness and of stupidity. Above all, the God of Péguy is a loving father to his coeternal son, and to his other sons and daughters in whom he sees his only-begotten.

Péguy turns a lot of conventional wisdom on its head, by trying to imagine things from God's point of view. This is, I think, a healthy counterweight to our modern temptation to regard God as so totally "other" that he becomes vague, alien, and unavailable— the temptation to look down at popular piety as childish and anthropomorphic. Péguy reminds us that we are able to imitate Christ because he first "imitated" us in becoming human. He who had made us in his image also assumed the whole human condition to reclaim and redeem it.

In Péguy's great poems, hope is something passed on from generation to generation, as holy water used to be passed from fingertip to fingertip. Hope is itself a participation in the communion of the saints. In his own way, Péguy here echoes the teaching of St. Thomas Aquinas, who defined hope generically as a good difficult to obtain but made possible through the help of one's friends. Our foremost and greatest friend is the Blessed Trinity, but after that there are our other friends—the Virgin Mary, the angels and those saints of Paradise, known or unknown to us, with whom we have a mysterious affinity. We are also helped by the hope of those we have known in the flesh, those whose words and example sustain us in times of discouragement. These friends are the guarantee of the invisible but very real grace that keeps us going. They make our hope possible, as we make theirs, and so renew the face of the earth.

December 19, 2008

'AN INCOMPARABLE WOMAN'

In his 1631 papal bull *Pastoralis romani pontifices,* Pope Urban VIII (d. 1644) declared:

> In order...that these plants that are so harmful to the Church of God might not extend further, we have decreed that they be torn up by their roots.... We decide and decree, with Apostolic authority, that the lifestyle and statutes of the congregation of women and virgins of the so-called "Jesuits" are null and void from the very beginning and without any power and value. And in order to bring this about, with this same authority, we suppress and extinguish them in their roots, completely; we abolish them perpetually and abrogate them. And, in order that all the faithful consider them suppressed, we completely divest those of the aforementioned Congregation or Sect who held offices and responsibilities and we order, in virtue of holy obedience and, under pain of excommunication, that these persons live separately from one another, outside of the colleges and houses where they have lived until now.

Who was responsible for the "monstrosity" Urban condemned in such harsh terms?

Mary Ward was born on January 23, 1585, into a respected aristocratic Yorkshire family. This was during the reign of Queen Elizabeth I, when English Catholics were driven into hiding, persecuted, often martyred. Two of Ward's uncles had been implicated in the famous Gunpowder Plot—an attempted assassination of James I. In 1599, the family home was burnt to the ground by rioting mobs. Mary and her two sisters were rescued by their father, and Mary was sent to the house of Sir Ralph Babthom at Osgodby-Selby. It was there, at the age of fifteen, that she first felt the call of a religious vocation. She entered a monastery of the Poor Clares at Saint-Omer in northern France and was later sent as a lay sister to the Spanish Netherlands.

Ward's ambition was to return to England, where monasteries had been abolished, priests were not tolerated, and lay Catholics lived under constant suspicion. In 1606, she founded a monastery specifically for English women at Saint-Omer. The community's rule was well adapted to the needs of Catholics in England. It provided both structure and flexibility. The "English Ladies," as Ward's nuns were called, would not wear a habit or live in a cloister, and they would dedicate themselves to the education of Catholic children and to supporting the local Catholic population in whatever way they could. Ward was, in fact, inspired in all this by the Society of Jesus. Members of her new community were even disparagingly called the "Jesuitesses" in some circles. Like the Society of Jesus, Ward hoped her community would not depend on the local bishop but directly on the pope.

Ward's "rule" was, to say the least, controversial. It went against the statutes that the Council of Trent had established for women's religious congregations. These required that women religious live cloistered lives, wear a religious habit, pray the Divine Office, and submit to the local bishop. The idea of giving women some of the same apostolic responsibilities that belonged to the male clergy was seen as a radical departure from tradition. So was the proposal that the "English Ladies" be self-governing. In brief, the Ladies were proposing a new form of religious life that threatened male supremacy.

Not all the popes were as opposed to Ward as Urban VIII. In fact, Urban's predecessors Paul V and Gregory XV had both supported her. Nor was Pope Urban as hostile toward Ward as the strong language of his 1631 bull might suggest (that was the conventional style of bulls back then). Still, after the promulgation of *Pastoralis romani pontifices*, Ward was imprisoned in Munich, in the convent of the Poor Clares. She was accused by the Inquisition of being a heretic and a schismatic (charges also leveled at Joan of Arc). When Urban learned of this, however, he ordered Ward's release and summoned her to Rome. There, the same pope who had suppressed Ward's order in northern France allowed her to open a new house for her community. She was not, however, allowed to leave the city until nearer the end of her life; nor was she to be recognized as the founder of her community. (The ensuing events are hard to follow because, after the suppression, efforts were made to destroy all the related documents.)

The times were, in fact, exceptional and rapidly changing. The antagonism between the English throne and the Catholic Church was aggravated by the papal excommunication of Queen Elizabeth and the release of her Catholic subjects from any oath of fidelity they might have made to her. In response, Elizabeth ratcheted up the persecution of English Catholics, who were suspected of plotting the overthrow of the queen. The Catholic Church in England was reduced to a mainly clandestine existence.

Ward, who had done all that she could to preserve what was left of the Catholic Church of England, obeyed the orders of Urban VIII without protesting and accepted the dissolution of her communities, whose members either returned to their families or entered recognized religious institutions. Under the patronage of the local nobility, some members of Ward's "institute" in the Catholic countries of the mainland continued their work of education for Catholic girls and outreach to the marginalized. They lived in "companionship and discernment," without the benefit of a religious rule and without being recognized as a "religious order." In 1637, Ward was finally allowed to return to England where houses were established in London and Heworth, near York. The latter was the first convent to be founded in England since the dissolution of the monasteries in 1536. Ward would remain there, an apparent failure, until her death in 1645.

Throughout her life, Mary Ward gave proofs of utmost fidelity to the Catholic Church and to the pope, even when he attempted to eradicate all she was striving to do. She was opposed by a group of clerics who were obsessed with the niceties of canon law, as well as by those who were hostile to the innovations of the Jesuits. Even some Jesuits opposed her, on the grounds that St. Ignatius had never wanted to establish a Society of Jesus for women. Finally, Ward had to contend with all those who thought it "unnatural" for women to abandon the tasks ordinarily associated with their sex.

After her death, Ward's companions carried on her work. Even though the institute had been officially suppressed and therefore had no official status as a religious congregation, its members found ways of keeping it alive. It wasn't until 1703 that Pope Clement XI approved a "rule" for the community. Pius IX subsequently recognized it as a religious institute. Today the Sisters of the Institute of the Blessed Virgin Mary (or the Sisters of Loreto—so called because of Mary's devotion to the Holy House of Loreto) number about seven hundred and are dispersed throughout the world. In addition to teaching children, the sisters have literacy programs for adults, give spiritual direction and counseling, provide shelters for the homeless, and participate in movements for greater justice in the world. The rule they were finally allowed to adopt included the wearing of the habit, but it also tried to incorporate the spirit of Ward's intuitions.

In 1951, Pius XII referred to Mary Ward as "an incomparable woman"; John Paul II spoke of her as "a pilgrim of hope." She was declared Venerable by Pope Benedict XVI in 2009. Ward's trajectory seems to demonstrate an axiom in church history: it is often those who suffer humbly and patiently from the church's contradictions who end up redeeming it, and sometimes also reforming it. Through her obedience and fidelity both to the church and to her own intuitions, Mary Ward ultimately brought about a radical change, opening new possibilities for women in the church.

June 2020

UNLIKELY PROPHETS

The years just before and after World War II saw breakthroughs in theology that had a major impact on Vatican II. For centuries the church had been waging a defensive battle against the abuses of the Enlightenment, the challenges of the Reform, and the rise of the secular nation-state. Theology had been reduced to defending the status quo or nurturing a form of popular piety that would set Catholicism apart from rival versions of Christianity. The "new theology," which developed above all in France, upset the calm and stagnant waters of scholasticism. It sought both to respond to the challenges of the modern world and to return to the sources of Christian faith. A vital reevaluation took place in these years, and since then nothing has been the same.

With the distance and comfort of hindsight, this theological transition can appear straightforward, even inevitable. But Vatican II did not just "happen." It was the fruit of many related but rarely coordinated initiatives undertaken by flawed people who often bickered with one another. Each had his own intuitions, each his own ego and quirks. Yet many of them recognized that they were all traveling on the same road, and they sharpened their own thinking by confronting their fellow travelers.

In France, much of the movement for renewal began with laypeople. A generation of lay mystics, artists, poets, and philosophers gradually created the spiritual and intellectual climate that would allow the "new theology" to flourish. Renewal came from the bottom—and seemed stuck there for a long time—before it was finally recognized as a gift of the Spirit to the church.

Among the first and most important figures in this movement was the writer Léon Bloy (1846–1917), the self-proclaimed "Pilgrim of the Absolute." Bloy thundered against the mediocrity of comfortable Christians and the "enlightened" bourgeoisie—and thus condemned himself to a life of extreme poverty and suffering. An autodidact who depended heavily on intuition, Bloy believed that the mysteries of faith surpass all understanding. He did not pretend to resolve the paradoxes and enigmas of Christianity; he simply proclaimed them.

Bloy owed his own conversion to an idiosyncratic cast of characters. There was Ernest Hello, a sickly lawyer who never practiced law and wrote books that almost no one read. There was Jules Amédée Barbey d'Aurevilly, a dandy who played at being an aristocrat and presented himself as a Catholic writer despite a scandalous private life. There was Auguste Villiers de l'Isle-Adam, a penniless bohemian who claimed to be the rightful owner of the island of Malta because one of his ancestors had been the Grand Master of the Knights of Malta. These laymen—each in his own way—affirmed the grandeur of Catholicism in the face of a society that had relegated religion to the sacristies. Precisely because they were not of the clerical establishment, and therefore not under its control, they were able to challenge both society and the church in an original way.

Bloy, too, was a sign of contradiction. Good at making both friends and enemies, he left no one indifferent. It was through Bloy that Jacques and Raïssa Maritain first discovered a Christian faith that wasn't an abstraction but rather an intense engagement. Before their conversion, the Maritains had made a suicide pact: they would search for a meaning in life more satisfactory than the one afforded by the then-prevailing scientism; and if, at the end of a year, they hadn't found one, they would end their lives. Their search led them first to Henri Bergson, whose critique of scientific determinism they found persuasive. Bergson's philosophy made human freedom and some kind of faith seem possible; Bloy's personal example made Christian faith seem both beautiful and necessary.

Shortly after the Maritains were baptized, with the Bloys as their godparents, another close friend of the Maritains announced his conversion. Charles Péguy, a militant socialist and poet, had a style and background very different from Bloy's, but his intuitions were strikingly similar. The Maritains tried to bring Bloy and Péguy together, but neither wanted anything to do with the other. Bloy was a monarchist, Péguy a man of the Left. So great was their political disagreement that neither would even read the other's works. By a strange irony, Bloy died in a house where Péguy had once lived. Bloy is considered by some to be at the origin of the modern "Catholic novel." What is certain is that Georges Bernanos, one of the most famous Catholic novelists of the twentieth century, discovered his vocation as a writer by reading Léon Bloy in the trenches during World War I. Péguy's work would exercise an important influence on the poet and playwright Paul Claudel; and on Emmanuel Mounier, the founder of the magazine *Esprit*, whose "personalist" philosophy developed some of Péguy's ideas.

The Maritains were not the only ones Bloy helped to convert. There were also Pierre and Christine van der Meer, Georges Roualt, Pierre Temier, and many others. It was the Maritains, however, who brought together a small informal community of artists and philosophers, some already converts, some still searching for God. Jacques Maritain was a philosopher, Raïssa a poet, but both were essentially mystics.

Jacques Maritain and Etienne Gilson are both closely associated with the neo-Thomist revival of the twentieth century. For them, the scholasticism that was being taught in seminaries was a closed and stagnant system, and a betrayal of the true spirit of St. Thomas Aquinas. The dynamism and depth of Aquinas's thought were not reducible to a simple list of propositions. Aquinas's philosophy could not be separated from his theology, and both pointed beyond themselves toward ineffable mysteries.

By its own inner logic, neo-Thomism also brought an opening to other religions and cultures. Louis Massignon and Louis Gardet dedicated themselves to the study of Islam, Olivier Lacombe to Hinduism. They tried to see the other as the other wished to see himself, according to what was purest and noblest in his tradition. There was nothing syncretistic about this approach; for Massignon, Gardet, and Lacombe, Christianity remained the measuring stick for all other religious traditions.

Another development that had a great impact on French Catholics in this period was the arrival of Russian intellectuals fleeing the Bolshevist revolution. The Russian Orthodox Church had itself been experiencing a renewal led by the laity. It involved writers and intellectuals such as Dostoevsky and Soloviev near the end of the nineteenth century and culminated in the 1917–18 Council of Moscow, which provided for massive lay participation at all levels of church governance (a reform never implemented because of the revolution).

These exiled Russians discovered what Nicolai Berdyaev would call "secret France"—the church of Bloy and Péguy, with its fools-for-Christ mysticism—and many of them recognized its similarities with their own religious tradition. Etienne Gilson's lectures about the need to return to the sources of medieval thought inspired some Russian philosophers and theologians to undertake the same kind of return to the fathers of the church, and to distinguish between Tradition and traditions, between what was vital truth and what was historical deadwood. This, in turn, sparked a revival of interest in the church fathers on the part of Catholic theologians such as Jean Daniélou and Henri de Lubac. *Ressourcement*, the return to the sources, began gaining momentum. The Orthodox-Catholic dialogue, unofficial and discreet, was enriching both churches at a subterranean level.

It is hard even to call this development a movement, since those associated with it moved in so many different directions. The Russian immigrants included czarists and socialists, both continuing their own little civil war on French soil. There were those who emphasized the uniqueness (and superiority) of Slavic culture and those who were more open to Western influences; those who emphasized a return to the church fathers and those who sought to reinterpret their traditions using the insights of contemporary philosophy. Their attitudes toward the mother church in Moscow varied greatly and produced bitter divisions that still persist.

Alongside the neo-Thomists were Catholic existentialists such as Gabriel Marcel, and even among the neo-Thomists there were tensions about what was essential and what was historically and culturally irrelevant in the synthesis of the "Angelic Doctor."

Some of the champions of what came to be called *la nouvelle théologie* were traditionalists, looking to the Middle Ages for a model of the ideal Christian society and leaning toward a sort of Christian fascism as their hope for the future. (Most of these fascist sympathies dissolved rather quickly when World War II broke out.) Many also had scandalous secrets. Some were openly homosexual; others were involved in extramarital affairs. Alongside authentic mysticism, there often existed a fascination with the paranormal and the apocalyptic. Many were intolerant of any ideas that were not their own and dismissed less zealous, more conventional Catholics as "bourgeois."

All these unlikely and quarrelsome prophets, with all their obvious shortcomings and vulnerabilities, somehow played a part in the renewal that would find full expression in Vatican II. The early church must have been something like this—with its different communities, each with its own concerns, its bitter rivalries and competing factions. The Apostles themselves didn't always get along with one another. Yet somehow the gospel went out from Jerusalem to the ends of the world. The story of how French Catholicism renewed itself in the first half of the twentieth century has a lesson relevant to Christians in any era, including our own. We really don't know the part each of us is playing in the construction of the Kingdom—perhaps in spite of ourselves.

December 18, 2009

JOURNET'S BLIND SPOT

On Saturday mornings, Charles Journet (more commonly known simply as Abbé Journet), would take the train from Fribourg to Geneva to teach a course on church history. He would usually stay overnight in Geneva and celebrate the 11 a.m. Mass at Sacred Heart Church—until the local bishop put a stop to that. Although some people came from far away to listen to Journet's hour-long sermons, the locals of the parish found that his Masses were much too long and complained about it. If Journet was hurt by the bishop's decision, he didn't let it show. In fact, he seemed oblivious to whatever concerned only himself. In those years just before the Second Vatican Council, Journet was among the most prominent intellectuals in the church, but you wouldn't know it from the way he presented himself; there wasn't a self-important bone in his body. He was the founding editor of the review *Nova et Vetera*, which was recognized as one of the better theological journals, and he was a close friend of the famous philosopher Jacques Maritain and his wife Raïssa. Journet was in his seventies when I first met him. He was one of several professors of dogmatic theology at the seminary of Fribourg, but he interacted very little with his colleagues and didn't make much of an impression on most of his students. He was very hard of hearing and that contributed to his isolation.

Abbé Journet would always arrive promptly for our classes, even when the weather was bad. A thin wisp of a man, he was bald, wore very thick glasses, and spoke with a delightful sing-song Swiss accent. He was still quite spry and would begin the classes by reciting the *Veni Creator* on his knees. There were only about twenty of us in the class, but it was obvious that he had carefully prepared his material. I was impressed by the intensity of his delivery; he put himself heart and soul into what he was trying to communicate. Often, he would pause and say with a naïve and authentic wonderment: "Isn't that beautiful, isn't that marvelous?" And, coming from him, it usually was.

He spoke of simple things with great depth and penetration. His history of the church was bathed in the light of his central intuition: The church is holy, pure, without sin, and its boundaries pass through our hearts. Whatever is pure in us, in all of human history, belongs to the church; whatever is sordid remains outside of it. It is impossible to love God without also loving the church, for the two are united as a bride to her bridegroom. Our own membership in the church militant is partial and fragile and, ultimately, a mystery. The hierarchical structure of the church is a gift of God, and this too should be loved and respected. The corollary is that whenever we use the church's authority to prophesy in our own name and justify our own ambitions, we have nothing to do with the true church of Christ. But even such abuses would eventually lead to a greater good and a purer truth.

I'm very grateful for all I received from Abbé Journet. Later, I would read his great work *The Church of the Incarnate Word*—his unfinished magnum opus, which I found luminous. We had only one private meeting and that was in Toulouse. He was staying in a small cottage not far from where Jacques Maritain lived. I can't recall why I was invited to have tea with him on an Easter Sunday afternoon. It had rained heavily that morning and the grass around his cottage was still very wet. I arrived on my bike, a bit late, pedaling furiously. Approaching the cottage, I slammed on the brakes, but they failed: I crashed into the door of Journet's cottage at full speed. As I sat there, contemplating the ruins of my bike, I heard a sing-song voice from within the cottage: "Come right in!" The partially deaf Abbé Journet thought I had simply knocked on the door. I don't recall much of the ensuing conversation except that he had a hard time deciphering my accent. I'd talk about one thing for a while and then he'd talk about something else.

When Paul VI named Abbé Journet a cardinal, everyone was stunned. Abbé who? He wasn't a bishop; he wasn't even a pastor. He was hardly known outside a small circle, and his own bishop barely tolerated him. No one was more stunned than Journet himself. It took nearly a week to convince him that he had to accept. It was

Maritain who finally persuaded him that this was not a personal honor but a way of honoring St. Thomas Aquinas and the neo-scholastic movement. Paul VI also had to reassure Abbé Journet (as he insisted on being called even after he was named cardinal) that he could continue to teach at Fribourg and would need to get dressed up in red only for very official ceremonies.

Vatican II was now in progress. I didn't follow the council very closely. I was in Latin America, facing other challenges, discovering, to my great disappointment, just how closely the Catholic hierarchy had come to identify itself with brutal political regimes. I was in Chile when the Pinochet coup took place; I saw the dirty war in Argentina and the "cocaine coup" in Bolivia. In almost all the conflicts in Latin America, most bishops supported the dictatorships du jour. I heard a few rumors about Abbé Journet being a wet blanket at the council. I later learned that these rumors were quite true—that Journet was agonizing about the changes that were taking place. There was evidently a side of him that had not been apparent in the classroom. Journet's reservations at the council struck me as ironic. It was the very principles I learned from him that opened me up to all sorts of new possibilities, giving me a sense of great freedom even as they anchored and broadened my love for the church. Nothing noble and holy was a stranger to the church; no truth, however partial, was alien to it, for all that was good was the fruit of the Holy Spirit, and the Holy Spirit was the life of the church. Yet for Abbé Journet, it became apparent, all that was not pure truth was dangerous. There was an intolerance for any sort of "deviation," for any questioning of the church's structures or hierarchical authority. Abbé Journet seemed locked into a formula. He was very suspicious of the ecumenical movement in all its forms. He refused to have anything to do with Taizé or any other group devoted to dialogue. Part of this is understandable. He grew up in Switzerland, where Catholics were often a persecuted minority, and his earliest publications were apologetical works. These controversies of his younger days seemed to have marked him definitively. He was critical of modern theologians—of Rahner, Zendel, Congar, and, of course, Hans Küng.

In retrospect, I think Journet's strengths were his weaknesses. He loved the Truth with passion—not as something he possessed but as Someone who possessed him as he was, with his own personality and idiosyncrasies. There's an old Thomistic axiom, "Whatever is received is received according to the mode of the recipient": each person's particular character colors his or her perceptions, and character is partly the effect of circumstance. Abbé Journet was an intellectual and a loner, a seminary professor during most of his active life. His milieu was a clerical milieu, which was still linked to the upper classes of society. Journet's "apostolate" consisted mainly in preaching retreats to nuns and groups of people who were cultivated and well-to-do. This is not to imply that he was on the side of the rich and powerful. His personal poverty was extreme and authentic; he preached and lived the evangelical virtues. He was not afraid to oppose the Swiss government and even his own bishop during World War II for their discreet collaboration with the Nazis in the name of "national interest." The only "power" he was interested in was the power of truth. But he was perhaps too quick to dismiss unfamiliar manifestations of the truth, which can offer itself to us under various disguises—as an ordinary traveler met on the road or a gardener at the tomb, as a humiliated prophet whom Pilate could not recognize. The title of the review Journet founded, *Nova et Vetera* ("Things Old and New"), evokes the Gospel parable of the scribe versed in the Kingdom of God and defines the program of the review. Abbé Journet did indeed bring forth new insights from old concepts, but he was less adept at bringing new insights to bear on old concepts, which is a different thing. Pope Leo XIII had given Thomism the church's official endorsement in *Aeterni Patris* (1879), and Journet was worried about any development within the church that might threaten Thomism's preeminence.

Journet, Maritain, and Paul VI formed a sort of troika of like-minded neo-Thomists who seemed to be overwhelmed by the scope and implications of the proposals of the council; they feared that things were spinning out of control. An old order was being abolished and there was genuine confusion and apprehension about what would replace it. Many lost their footing. Was this a valid excuse to rein things in? My own experience of Abbé Journet leads me to believe that the answer is not simple. What set St. Thomas apart was his ability to assimilate all forms of truth, whatever their source, and incorporate them into a dynamic synthesis. In this, he was continuing the works of the great fathers of the church, who incorporated the insights and categories of pagan philosophies and mysticism in their effort to better know and love the self-revealing God—and his ultimate revelation in the Incarnate Word. This is an ongoing process. Journet would not have denied this in theory, yet in practice he seemed to resist anything outside of his own theological scheme. Such rigidity risked making neo-Thomism irrelevant in the wake of the council. In contrast to this narrowness, we have John Paul II in the chapter titled "Why Divided?" in his book *Crossing the Threshold of Hope*:

> Why would the Holy Spirit have permitted so many different divisions and enmities among those who claim to be disciples of the same Gospel, disciples of the same Christ?... There are two possible answers to this question. The more negative one would see in these divisions the bitter fruit of sins committed by Christians. The more positive answer is inspired by trust in the One who is capable of bringing forth good from evil, from human weakness. Could it not be that these divisions have also been *a path continually leading the church to discover the untold wealth contained in Christ's Gospel and in the redemption accomplished in Christ?* Perhaps all this wealth would not have come to light otherwise.... It is necessary *for humanity to achieve unity through plurality, to learn to come together in the one church, even while presenting a plurality of ways of thinking and acting, of cultures and civilizations.* Wouldn't such a way of looking at things be, in a certain sense, more consonant with the wisdom of God, with his goodness and providence?

The neo-Thomism of Journet and Maritain still has much to recommend it; it rescued the basic intuitions of St. Thomas from the shallow scholasticism that had obscured them, and those intuitions are as valuable today as they were before the council. But Journet was as suspicious of theological innovation—as ill-disposed toward the distinctive intuitions of the modern world—as the unreconstructed scholastics had been of the neo-Thomists. The same syndrome is visible among some of Journet's theological descendants, but it is not irreversible. Thomism is adaptive and resourceful; it will always survive the anxieties and blind spots of rearguard Thomists.

December 20, 2013

THE CHILEAN COUP: AN EYEWITNESS REPORT

*(The following is a foundry worker's first-hand account of events
surrounding the September 11, 1973 coup in Chile. The author, who
managed to escape into Argentina where he wrote this, had to remain
anonymous, but was well known to the Division for Latin America,
U.S. Catholic Conference, which verified his account.)*

SEPTEMBER 11, 1973. At 1 p.m. the last group of workers that
refused to take advantage of the trucks put at our disposal to take
us home left the factory for a rallying point. We had a long march
ahead of us to reach that point on the outskirts of Santiago. Public
transport had ceased, and the streets were full of frightened people
trying to get to safety before the 3 p.m. curfew.

In the distance the Moneda, presidential palace, was smoking
and planes still circled above our heads. Sergio had filled a sack with
bread and baked beans left over from the canteen; nobody had felt
much like eating at noon. Before passing the gate, we destroyed our
papers...and a part of ourselves.

In groups of two or three we began the long march across the
city trying to avoid the rapidly improvised controls. We tried to look
natural, like we were enjoying all this, clenching fists to control the
desire to weep from frustration and helplessness.

In one or another middle-class section we passed through, the
reactionaries were celebrating. Bread and sugar and oil, which had
long since disappeared from the market, were being distributed in
the streets...The Marxist tyranny had been overthrown and there
was now everything for everybody. Manuel, Jorge and I spoke very
little, just a few muttered curses from time to time. We had plenty of
time to think. We got through a roadblock by pure luck.

When the Unidad Popular won the 1970 elections, I wasn't sure
what to expect. In Popular neighborhoods, the people danced in
the streets and wept for joy. A great aspiration and hope were born;
but I had my doubts. For those born and bred in a capitalist society,

Marxism means repression, violence, persecution. Moreover, the professional politicians of the left didn't impress me too much either. They greatly resembled their right-wing counterparts. A three-year experience led me to modify a lot of these first judgments.

In the months following the elections, there was no repression: quite the contrary. Even the public functionaries, ordinarily dismissed when there was a change of government, were maintained in office; new posts were created for the new personnel. If the major national and international trusts were quickly expropriated—generally with an ample compensation—the small and medium industries were left untouched. The middle class was courted and offered guarantees. The violence was purely verbal, directed against the old system and the priorities of a privileged class.

It was the working class that most benefited in the beginning. My factory, left bankrupt after the boss' trip to Europe "to see his family" six months before the election, was taken over by the state to avoid its shut-down. Wages were at once tripled and a worker participation system was put in. The change was impressive.

The workers, who before wouldn't dare speak up to a boss, were given the opportunity to express themselves, to control the destiny of their plant, its production plan, its finances. They were given a sense of their dignity and possibilities as a class. All in all, it worked pretty good. In August we had broken all production records, in spite of difficulties getting raw materials. We calculated that in another year we'd be able to double our production, modernize our plant, and begin to produce in Chile many items that until now were imported.

As we trudged on in silence, all that now seemed so naive, ingenuous. It was the end of a hope, the end of an ideal. There's a type of spiritual death more bitter and deep than the physical one. We'll never know how many persons died around us that day...but all those deaths were as symbols of something that was killed inside of a people.

Unless we're completely cynical, we all tend to see other people as well-intended as ourselves and calculate their reactions after our own. I guess that was one of the big mistakes of the Unidad Popular, all the verbalism notwithstanding. Allende promised to respect the actual Constitution, the reigning legality, the Congress, even though these consecrated a certain type of society and protected the interests of the upper classes.

Allende sincerely believed that he could convince a great sector of the middle and upper class to integrate their interests in a common good, to subordinate privileged interests to the general welfare and, above all, to the welfare of the working class. To such an end a complete liberty was given to the opposition. Their institutions were respected; sooner or later they would see the light.

What was practiced by Allende was reflected by the workers. The few workmates who resisted the changes were considered as "mistaken," but they were by no means excluded. They were our companions of class, worthy of confidence. But they were the same persons who after the *golpe* drew up the lists denouncing the "Marxists" among their fellow workers, sending them to unemployment and prison.

Without pretending to label the two political camps as sons of light and sons of darkness, I can honestly state that there was a difference of moral level.

Some people, especially the Military Junta, have accused the Marxist government of fomenting hatred and division among Chileans. But the vital element in Chilean socialism wasn't hatred or division; it was a true and real love that aspired to an authentic unity.

If we define love as the desire for the authentic good of the other, such a love will express itself differently according to whether it's directed toward the oppressed or toward the oppressor. The authentic good of the oppressor is that he cease to oppress. The other face of this love is the Christian duty to hate the sin of social and economic oppression that opposes itself to the real welfare of the person and society. The breaking down of barriers which divide people into classes is the only way to a *real* unity.

Opposed to this love which desires the good of the other is the egoism that defends one's own benefits and privileges and that hates whatever threatens these advantages. I'm convinced that the events speak for themselves in the Chilean experience. The moral quality of the present repression and terrorism is, quite simply, the expression of a real egotistical hatred. Behind the pompous pronouncements of the Military can be discerned something satanic.

Allende no sooner took control of government when, in the name of liberty and democracy, the counterattack began. Credits from the capitalist countries were drastically reduced, and those credits that were extended were essentially destined for high-cost consumer goods and the preservation of economic dependency. The credits provided by socialist countries were for productive goods which would have permitted Chile a steady economic growth with relative autonomy.

The upper and middle classes, whose representatives controlled Congress, systematically vetoed the decrees which aimed for a redistribution of the national income. Periodic graduated wage increases, offered by the government to offset the rise in the cost of living and the loss of purchasing power of the working class, were approved. But their proposed financing, through taxes on luxury items and excessively high incomes, was rejected. The wage adjustments thus contributed to the inflation. It was a vicious circle.

Once the opposition had consolidated its resources, the final assault began. The truck-owners struck. This strike didn't begin forty days before the *golpe*...It had been going on as a systematic sabotage for a long while, protected by the "democratic" institution, i.e., the Congress and the courts. Attempts on the part of drivers, workers and farmers to move the trucks were met with violence and terrorism from the rightist paramilitary groups. Food transport to markets was cut off, as were raw materials to factories. The shop-owners joined in and did their part to create a black market and help it flourish. Doctors and professionals struck. Santiago was laid siege by hunger. Life was becoming nearly impossible.

The working class sought to meet the crisis with its basic arms: its patience, courage and tenacity. But getting to work was a battle; getting home was worse. At work there was little or no raw material. Food was so scarce that the bread lines would begin at daybreak—

and oftentimes wind up in brawls. It was an uneven match.

Of course, all the blame was thrown on the "incompetence of the Marxist government." Only a fanatic would deny that there were abuses and errors—political posts, indeed, were often filled by incompetent personnel; on a certain level there was a good deal of sectarianism (though that sin was officially labeled as such and denounced); and the moral conduct of many professional politicians was totally inconsistent with their "revolutionary" engagement. But the blame frequently rested elsewhere. On the whole the people really responsible for the economic and social chaos were the least affected by the chaos. The poor were, however; the poor always pay the price.

We got to the rallying point just at curfew time. The response had been pretty good: about 500 workers from a zone where there were very few industries. The only news was from the military radio station. It was cold, beginning to rain. We huddled together in a tent and passed around a cup of tea and pieces of bread, wondering what the hell we were going to do. A helicopter hovered over us. We observed its movements through the holes in the tent. Machine-guns echoed in the distance. A few bombs exploded.

We were full of sadness, chagrin and helplessness, but not afraid. We stayed tuned to the radio station broadcasting official news and official decrees. We sometimes felt like crying, sometimes like laughing; hypocrisy, when it gets to a certain point, becomes ridiculous.

A day or two before the *golpe*, a group of society women had organized a march on the Defense Ministry to demand military intervention to overthrow the government. Moreover, the political parties of the opposition—"bastions of democracy"—had been preparing the Armed Forces for this end. Paramilitary right-wing groups had been supporting the truck-owners' strike by blowing up bridges and railroad tracks, and sniping at the few convoys seeking to bring food to the capital and raw material to the factories.

The week before the *golpe* we ran out of ingots for the foundry. After hijacking a few trucks, which we incorporated into a larger convoy, we asked for volunteers from among the workers to accompany the trucks to the city of Concepcion. Just about everyone offered himself and it was a difficult job of selecting people. The convoy left Santiago on Wednesday and got back Sunday night. Our companions, who didn't claim overtime or bonuses, had to load and unload the trucks, sleep in them and go without eating—for they'd left only with the money they had in their pockets. The snipers picked off three men in the convoy...None was from our factory, though one of our trucks returned riddled with bullets. The men were at their posts, haggard and bleary-eyed, Monday morning to prepare the molds for casting on Tuesday.

On Tuesday, September 11, at 11 p.m., we had to empty the furnace without casting. The Moneda was being bombed...

With the military controlling all sources of information it was hard to figure out in our tent just what was going on. There were rumors of uprisings within the troops of certain regiments supporting Allende, but it was difficult to form a correct idea of the alignment of forces and, in consequence, to determine a plan of action. The resistance in certain sectors was based on these rumors. If it were true that a part of the troops was loyal to Allende and actually engaged in battle, then a worker resistance, even with their very limited means, could have swung the balance. As it turned out these rumors were greatly exaggerated. Resistance would have been suicide.

WEDNESDAY, SEPTEMBER 12. The Armed Forces issued an ultimatum summoning all the resisters to surrender themselves before 3 p.m. Most, realizing that their situation was hopeless, did so. Others who didn't were executed on the spot. We spent two days of indecision before accepting the fact that the cause was lost, that active resistance was useless and that a new phase of our life was to begin.

The witch-hunt began almost at once. The "patriotic citizens" were invited to denounce "suspicious elements." Whole neighborhoods were searched, oftentimes with extreme violence and terrible humiliations. In the factories, lists were drawn up of "Marxists," and these workers were immediately suspended. "Foreigners" were a particular target, especially those who had fled to Chile to escape the persecution of other Latin American fascist governments. The purge had been sweeping on.

In the National Stadium more than two weeks after the *golpe,* there are still several thousand prisoners. There are many rumors of massive assassinations, detentions and tortures. If a tenth part of these rumors is true, this is the worst massacre in the history of the continent.

Our jobs were gone, of course. Along with a large number of workmates we had to move about with great caution, with the threat of prison or worse hanging over our heads. We escaped—with hope intact...and our ideals too. There's something in our hearts that bullets can't kill and prison and torture can't intimidate. The experience of a real freedom, and a real democracy, a new type of solidarity in sacrifice and in an ideal...a solidarity which tended to surpass economic, social, cultural and even national differences. This experience will never die.

Indeed, we are stronger than ever...the blood of martyrs is the seed of a new world. Nothing and no one can prevent this seed from springing up to fuller life. *Hasta la victoria final.*

November 2, 1973

ARTIST, ACTIVIST, MARTYR

Outside of Bolivia, I don't think many people knew of Luis Espinal before Pope Francis, during his 2015 visit to that country, stopped to pray at the site where Espinal's body, riddled with bullets and showing signs of torture, had been found in a landfill. Evo Morales, Bolivia's first indigenous president, gave the pope a replica of a wooden crucifix that Luis had sculpted; it portrays Christ nailed to a hammer and sickle. This seemed a clumsy and controversial gesture, to say the least, implying that Espinal, an icon in the country's struggle for democracy, was in fact a secret Marxist who would have supported Morales. This, at any rate, was the impression I had from the way the incident was presented by the media. I was disconcerted at first. This was not at all the Luis Espinal I knew.

I lived in Bolivia for five years and got to know "Lucho" Espinal fairly well. In fact, he is one of the godfathers of my son. In a corridor of our house hangs a wooden sculpture by Luis depicting the head and arms of the crucified Christ. Christ appears to be in a peaceful yet somehow painful sleep, all absorbed in his work of redemption. It wasn't hard to get to know Luis: he was a very simple and unpresuming person who always seemed to be available to anyone. At that time, he was known mostly as a film critic and taught communications at the Catholic University of La Paz. His main interest was the media. He lived with two other Jesuits in a very simple dwelling in one of the poorer districts of La Paz.

To understand Luis, it is important to situate him in the context of his times. The day I arrived in La Paz in 1974, the big news was that Hugo Banzer's government had ordered the suppression of the Justice and Peace Commission of the Bolivian bishops' conference. The priest in charge of the commission was expelled from the country. The church, accused of fomenting social unrest and encouraging subversion, was deeply divided. The Bolivian Constitution still recognized Catholicism as the official religion, and the state promised to favor and protect it. (This changed some years later, when Bolivia became a secular state after a referendum.) In return for this privileged status, the church had the obligation to cooperate with and support the state. Under Banzer, the military ruled by decrees; political parties and trade unions were banned. The Justice and Peace Commission was the only organization that had dared to criticize the government. With its suppression, tranquility was restored—but it was the tranquility of a graveyard. A large part of the clergy and hierarchy were satisfied with this: as long as they behaved and stuck to administering the sacraments and overseeing popular devotions, they were considered to be doing God's work and had it pretty good. But underneath it all, there was deep frustration and humiliation. Elements of the clergy were shocked by the dismal conditions and thousand little tyrannies to which the people were submitted. Many foreign priests, in particular, were unaccustomed to dealing with such situations and felt they could not cooperate with policies and practices so offensive to simple human dignity. Luis was Spanish but totally devoted to the poor of Bolivia; he had renounced his Spanish citizenship and was a naturalized Bolivian.

A turning point came in 1978 when Adolfo Pérez Esquivel, the future Nobel Peace Prize recipient, visited La Paz. At that time, he was head of what was called the Peace and Justice Commission of Argentina, a human-rights advocacy group. He quietly proposed to set up a similar group in Bolivia. Jimmy Carter had been elected in the United States and was championing human rights; and it was widely felt that if we could put together an organization dedicated exclusively to human rights, the military would probably not dare to attack it. It was also important that such a group be totally independent of the church and its hierarchy. The new group would be a voice for the oppressed, their only voice. A few months later a delegate of Pérez Esquivel came to La Paz and helped us organize. He did a remarkable job: within a week the Permanent Assembly for Human Rights had become a reality. Luis was part of the project, but he was not offered a leadership role—nor would he have wanted one. That would have been totally out of character for him.

The new Human Rights Assembly set itself very modest goals at the beginning. It was not at all prepared when a group of women whose husbands had been jailed showed up and announced that they were going on a hunger strike and planned to install themselves in the bishop's residence. Members of the Assembly tried to dissuade the women, telling them it would be pointless at this stage of the game. The women's reply was simple: "We didn't come here looking for advice or even support. We are simply telling you what we are going to do whether you like it or not. Our husbands are in prison, we don't have anything to eat anyway so we might as well fast publicly." There were three women and perhaps ten children in the group. When, after a few days, it became obvious that this was very serious and the children still refused the food the bishop had sent them, ten members of the Assembly offered to replace the children, and this was accepted by the mothers. Luis was among those who offered themselves. The new group set up shop in the offices of *Presencia*, a Catholic daily newspaper, not particularly known for its opposition to the dictatorship. Hunger strikes soon began to break out all over the country. After about two weeks, the government broke into the newspaper offices and forcibly removed the hunger strikers. The authorities claimed they found plenty of food, liquor, and drugs on the premises, and that the whole thing was a farce. Unfortunately for the government, a television station, alerted to the raid, had the whole thing filmed and broadcast. The footage showed people being carried out on stretchers, too weak to walk and singing the Beatitudes. About a week later, Banzer announced that he was resigning, and that elections would be held.

The transition to democracy after years of a totalitarian dictatorship was not easy, and for a long time the situation was chaotic. During that period, Luis launched a weekly newspaper called *Aquí*, which was a voice of sanity and clarity in the middle of all the confusion. He continued to teach at the Catholic University. He was a poet and an artist, with a very acute sensitivity and a genuine love for the oppressed and humiliated. On March 21, 1980, he was kidnapped a few blocks from his house. Someone heard him cry, "This is it!"—as if he was expecting it. His body was found the next morning.

They say that after the death of Benedict Joseph Labre—a homeless beggar and mystic who lived among the ruins of the Roman Colosseum—the people of Rome proclaimed him a saint before he was even buried. Something similar happened to Luis. He was not particularly well known, not much of a public figure, but the whole city of La Paz shut down for his funeral. The largest crowd I'd ever seen accompanied Luis's body from the cathedral to the cemetery, some singing hymns and praying, others shouting political slogans. Luis had touched something deep in the hearts of the Bolivian people he loved so much, and they recognized their purest aspirations in him. Their affection and gratitude has not faded with the passage of time. Streets, markets, and schools have been named in his honor. You can't go far in La Paz without seeing his name.

Luis did not belong to any political party. Nor was he part of any organized "movement." He was a man of peace and dialogue. There was even something a bit timid about him; he never imposed himself and would render little services without being asked. There was an unmistakable purity in him, and this purity was truly revolutionary.

But it would not surprise me if, given the situation at the time, Luis had seen in Marxism Gospel values that were sorely lacking in certain sectors of the church, and believed that these values could and should be incorporated into a Christian vision of society. That he should have such sentiments seems almost natural. I had them myself at the time. In Latin America, Marxism took many forms; it was not identified only with the Communist Party. In fact, the bona fide Communist parties I knew in Latin America were little self-enclosed cliques with little popular support. There was a need for some sort of collaboration with what was best in the left-wing parties. That seemed indispensable if real change were to come about.

When Pope Francis was questioned about the "strange" gift of the "Marxist Christ," his response clarified the real significance of the sculpture. The pope, unlike myself, seems to have gotten it right away. Just as those who tried to live the Beatitudes were automatically branded "Marxists" by the powerful and comfortable, Christ too might have been crucified as a Marxist, branded with the stigma of the hammer and sickle, with all its connotations of hatred and destruction. It is a very powerful and provocative challenge. There are not lacking voices today, in this country and even in the church, similarly branding Pope Francis a "Marxist" (for example, Rush Limbaugh). Archbishop Romero was assassinated two days after Luis for being a "Marxist"; Dorothy Day was considered a Communist; Thomas Merton, a subversive. Time has shown them to be prophets, ahead of their time. "By their fruits shall you know them."

What Pope Francis, the "Marxist pope," is doing for the church is the stuff Luis dreamed of. And I think that Pope Francis, who certainly knew Luis, is well aware of that. It was people like Luis who went to the peripheries and prepared the way.

August 14, 2015

THE NEWS THAT DIDN'T FIT

Reporting the June 1994 consistory of the College of Cardinals, the American media missed the point. Their main focus was on the assembly's endorsement of Pope John Paul II's approach to the then upcoming Cairo conference on population and development. The endorsement was highly predictable; more importantly, it was a sidebar to the consistory's main business: preparations for observing the passing of the second millennium and the beginning of the third. Further, the position paper on the observance, submitted to the cardinals with the authority of the pope, went beyond ceremony and deep into substance. The multi-faceted program outlined in the document, titled "Reflections on the Great Jubilee of the Year 2000," seriously complicates the stereotype of John Paul II as a reactionary intent on consolidating the past rather than facing the future.

Of the major points, the most surprising was a proposal that the church prepare for the third millennium through a serious examination of conscience, confessing the sins, errors of commission and omission, and even crimes committed by its representatives and in its name in the church's first 2,000 years. The project would be brought to realization prior to the Jubilee Year already proclaimed for the year 2000. It is very much in line with the efforts of the Second Vatican Council—particularly in the documents on religious liberty, ecumenism, and relations with Jews and other non-Christians— to shed the triumphalism of the past and to practice humility and contrition where the record demands it.

The proposal specifically cites the coercive methods used in the name of the Catholic faith in the wars of religion and during the Inquisition, describes these actions as crimes against humanity, puts them on the same footing with Hitlerism and Stalinism, and even finds a historical link: "The crimes of Hitler's Nazism and Marxist Stalinism arose from such coercive methods."

"Reflections" contains other shockers. It calls for an assembly, to be held on Mt. Sinai, of all the "sons of Abraham," represented by the leaders of Christianity, Judaism, and Islam, to affirm their common ancestry and the uniqueness of their God, renounce all violence among brothers, put aside antagonisms, and affirm the basic tenets of morality as given in the Decalogue.

Another proposal suggests a pan-Christian reunion at Bethlehem and Jerusalem, to be realized in collaboration with the World Council of Churches and the Great Council of Orthodoxy. The paper asks for a new martyrology which would include non-Catholics who have given their testimony of faith in Christ, among them the saints recognized by Orthodoxy and the martyrs of Protestantism. Echoing a frequent theme in Catholic publications, it also asks for the canonization of more lay people, including married people. The Second Vatican Council and the great popes of this century are credited in the document with preparing the way for the Jubilee Year.

The text also makes reference to the Galileo case and comments that further study may reveal "similar errors, or even faults, regarding the proper autonomy of science."

The paper tries to anticipate objections to acknowledgment of Catholic crimes. Such a confession of faults, it says, will not diminish but rather enhance the moral authority of the church by demonstrating a courageous commitment to truth. By implication, this spectacle of a penitent church on its knees, asking pardon of God and all his peoples for its infidelities, can be read as an invitation to individual Catholics to reexamine their own Catholicism and weed out from it any elements of self-righteousness and arrogance toward others, and an invitation to other religions to enter into a similar reevaluation of their conduct past and present.

Given the nature and scope of the program offered to the consistory, the failure of the American media, both Catholic and secular, to provide coverage is greatly puzzling. True, the content of the paper and the proceedings of the consistory were officially secret and as such have never been reported in *L'Osservatore Romano*. But the full text of the program was leaked to *Adista.DOC,* a fortnightly documentary service published in Rome, and the response within the consistory was described by an "audacious cardinal" to a writer for *II Regno Attualita,* a news magazine published by the Dehonian (Sacred Heart) Fathers in Bologna.

Since an American prelate, Cardinal John O'Connor of New York, served as point man on population issues during the consistory, it may be that journalistic preoccupation with personalities and local angles distracted reporters from a far bigger story that earned more coverage in other countries—though not, in this writer's opinion, as much as the news deserved. The event was brought to my attention by Jean François Nothomb, director of the Jacques Maritain Institute in Rome.

Another explanation for neglect of the story may be that Catholics in the U.S. are so obsessed with pressing "practical" issues—abortion, birth control, the role of women, church-state relations—that an effort to see the church in the context of its entire history, to embrace the transcendental dimensions of that history, and to do so in a deeply ecumenical spirit raises few echoes here. One can only hope that attention will be paid.

October 21, 1994

PRIVILEGE MASKED AS ORTHODOXY

On Pentecost Sunday 2018, Pope Francis named fourteen new cardinals. Several of those selected were from the "peripheries," countries where Christians are a small and vulnerable minority, such as Japan, Pakistan, Iraq, and Madagascar. The other new cardinals were members of the Curia or heads of national bishops' conferences. Three honorary members—too old to vote in a consistory—were also named: the Spanish Claretian spiritual writer Aquilino Bocos Merino; a retired bishop from Mexico, Sergio Obeso Rivera; and a retired Bolivian bishop few Catholics had heard of—Toribio Ticona Porco.

Ticona was bishop in the territorial prefecture of Corocoro, which is not even a real diocese. It includes a large mining district but no major population centers. In keeping with canon law, he offered his demission in 2012 when he turned seventy-five, and it was accepted. After his retirement, he dedicated himself to the foundation of a school for orphans. He is now suffering from Parkinson's disease.

The only thing Ticona is really noted for is his love for the poor. In fact, his whole life has been marked by poverty. He is a Quechua-speaking Indian whose father died at a young age after working in the mines. In his youth, Ticona helped support his family by shining shoes and selling newspapers. He lied about his age so that he could join the military early and so become less of a burden for his mother. After military service, he worked in the mines and then at a brewery for about five years. Through contact with Belgian missionaries, he first felt a vocation to the priesthood. He was sent to study at a seminary in Chile but that lasted only a few months; he had received a very sketchy formal education and was far behind his fellow seminarians. He was finally able to continue his studies back in Bolivia, where he had more support.

After ordination, Ticona was sent to a town in a mining district called Chacarilla. The town itself had a population of only twenty-three people, but the parish included the surrounding areas and the total number of parishioners was about two thousand. Given the circumstances, it was not all that surprising that the community of Chacarilla asked Ticona to serve as mayor, which he did for fourteen years. In 1986, Ticona was anointed auxiliary bishop of Potosí and also given responsibility for the Bolivian community in Buenos Aires, where he first met Jorge Bergoglio. In 1992 he was named bishop of Corocoro, where he served until his retirement.

Ticona is only the third Bolivian cardinal and his country's first indigenous one. He is not in the traditional image of a "prince of the church," an honor usually reserved for members of the nobility or leaders of important dioceses. But his selection is in line with Pope Francis's desire for a church of and for the poor, and with his call for pastors who are not foremen or feudal lords but servants, poor and simple, close to the people. Pastors with "the smell of sheep."

So far, so good. I thought Ticona's appointment as a cardinal deserved more attention and decided to try to write something about it. To get more information I searched for Toribio Ticona—the first entry I ran across was "New Cardinal Denies Having Wife and Children." Other entries echoed similar accusations. The principal source for all this information was a Spanish news agency, *Adelante la Fe*—one of the media outlets the former papal nuncio Carlo Maria Viganò used to publicize his letter asking Pope Francis to resign. According to *Adelante la Fe*, the pope was perfectly aware of Ticona's situation, and the message the pope wanted to send was that celibacy is no longer important in the church. This was simply another step in a systematic dismantling of essential structures, the "great apostasy" supposedly announced at Fatima. As I dug further into this story, I discovered a whole little world of traditionalist groups that were eagerly promoting it. Some of them claim to remain in communion with Rome, while others have entered into open schism.

Now, I can understand the nostalgia for Latin, for a certain lost "grandeur" and security, and I respect those who feel as though they need this. In fact, I have shared this nostalgia myself, and I think the church has shown a great deal of patience toward those who feel this way, as long as only incidentals are involved.

But what we are witnessing in many traditionalist groups of the kind that have targeted Ticona is on a different level altogether. Here Catholic identity is being defined as adherence to a rigid and unforgiving moral code and to a formalistic liturgical rite. This is combined with a total disregard and even disdain for social justice and the teachings of Vatican II. The image of a triumphant and glorious church is part of our creed and the object of our hope, but it is not our present reality, and to pretend otherwise is a dangerous form of self-deception. The Kingdom of Christ is not of this world; we are not yet a cortege of white-robed innocents following the Lamb wherever He goes. We are members of a pilgrim church, a community of broken people seeking mercy—and a communion of saints only to the degree that this mercy is received. Beneath all the triumphalism of the traditionalists can be heard the blasphemous prayer of the Pharisee: "I give you thanks, O Lord, that I am not like the rest of men."

Something of this mentality can be sensed in the defamation campaign against Toribio Ticona and Pope Francis. This shouldn't surprise or scandalize us too much. The image of the pilgrim church reflects the image of the pilgrim Christ, who was reviled and, finally, crucified. We are never more attuned to the spirit of Jesus and the church than when we are humiliated and ridiculed. Still, it is disappointing, to say the least, to see Ticona vilified in the press and used as a cudgel with which to attack the pope.

I spent six years in Bolivia and learned something about the country during that time. One thing I learned is that celibacy is all but meaningless for the indigenous culture. What it values is fecundity. I have been told that, during Vatican II, the Bolivian bishops actually requested that celibacy be optional for the indigenous clergy (they never received a response). The unofficial solution to this problem was to have a "housekeeper" in the rectory of rural parishes. This did not necessarily mean that the priest and his housekeeper were living as husband and wife, but it was an arrangement that the local people could accept: it meant that their wives and daughters were more or less safe. In many cases, this was the only way to make sure the people could trust their pastor. A celibate man, living alone, was commonly considered a strange and even dangerous freak. I knew a Belgian priest who lived in the south of Bolivia with a woman who was a member of a secular institute. This woman had adopted two Bolivian orphans, who called the priest "Daddy." Both the priest and the woman were loved and respected in the parish, and they loved and respected each other, but there was absolutely nothing sensual between them. This was one of the most impressive communities I've ever seen, and it would not have been possible for either of them alone. But what would someone from the outside, who did not understand the situation, think?

So, yes, it's quite conceivable that Ticona had such a "housekeeper," especially given his physical limitations. But even if he did (and no evidence has been produced), that wouldn't prove he had an illicit sexual relationship. To imagine it would be to ignore the local context and to interpret the situation according to standards that are irrelevant. These accusations against Ticona were first made in 2011; they were investigated by the Vatican and dismissed as calumnies. After the rumors resurfaced last year, Ticona publicly denied them, and threatened legal action against the media outlets responsible for spreading them.

It has also been reported by *Adelante la Fe* that the Bolivian bishops' conference has forbidden Ticona to speak in its name, mainly because of his relationship with the controversial Bolivian president, Evo Morales. The two are old friends (Morales is the country's first indigenous president), and Morales was there in Rome when Ticona received his red hat. Ticona has criticized President Morales for certain things but has refused to comment on others, insisting that this is not his role. He does hope for a closer and more fruitful relationship between the government and the church, but as far as I know he has never pretended to speak in the name of the bishops' conference. He has taken great pains to clarify that his political opinions are personal.

Adelante la Fe also claims that the Bolivian bishops have isolated Ticona because he is an "indigenist" who, in collaboration with Morales, wants to impose native cultural values on Bolivian society. Of course, the history of Bolivia is largely one of European cultural values being imposed by a minority on the native population. It has also been darkly alleged that the cardinal "did not always wear his clerical garb in public," and that he is in favor of liberation theology, which, for some traditionalist Catholics, is indistinguishable from Communism.

I have spoken with friends of mine in Bolivia, and apparently no one there takes these accusations against Ticona seriously except the people who make them. I find this all very sad. I know that "in my Father's house there are many mansions": there are different sensitivities, cultural values, political contexts. I know that we always have much to learn from those with whom we disagree; they can make us see our own weaknesses, and we should be grateful to them for that. There should be tolerance, humility, receptivity, and respect on all sides. And this is exactly what many arch-traditionalists expect from the church for themselves, while refusing to offer it to others. They demand to be indulged, even as they condemn the rest of us.

Still, character assassination needs to be called out by its name, and clearly contrasted with the Gospel. What should have been a moment for celebration—the elevation of an indigenous cardinal whose only distinction was his quiet service to the poor in a mostly forgotten corner of Latin America—instead became the occasion for another battle in the war against Pope Francis. To any outside observer, the defamation of Cardinal Ticona looks like a defense not of orthodoxy but of privilege: Ticona has the wrong politics, the wrong friends, the wrong background. One could fairly call this attitude anti-evangelical. Or one could just call it pathetic.

March 8, 2019

Other Voices

TWICE ON SUNDAYS: MY ORTHODOX TEMPTATION

According to the version my wife likes to tell, when she took me to see the house which was up for sale and with which she had fallen in love, I glanced at the place, shrugged my shoulders, and made some kind of disparaging remark. Then the Russian Orthodox church diagonally across the street caught my eye. I looked at it for a while, then turned back to my wife's dream house and decided it wasn't so bad after all.

That is, of course, a gross exaggeration. The real reason I agreed to buy the house was that my wife had already made up her mind about the matter and we had, from the beginning of our marriage, decided that she would have the responsibility for the minor decisions of the household (where we were going to live, what school the kid would attend, etc.), while I would take care of the more important issues (how to resolve the conflict in Bosnia, balance the national budget, etc.). That having been clarified, I'll admit that I was not indifferent to the proximity of Saint Mary's.

Aesthetically, Saint Mary's is a little jewel—a white wooden structure which just barely dominates the surrounding two-family dwellings with its cruciform layout and its two, light-gray onion-shaped domes surmounted by the cross of Saint Andrew. It reminded me of photos I had seen years ago of rural churches in Ukraine and Orthodox Poland. Nothing pretentious, a certain noble simplicity and purity. The interior is something else. The walls and partitions are plastered with icons worthy of Saint Sulpice, which had been donated to the church and hung up every which way without too much rhyme or reason. The church can accommodate about sixty people in the nave and is usually comfortably full for Sunday liturgies. A lot of the parishioners are elderly or late middle age, but there's also a generous sprinkling of younger folk and a certain number of non-Russian converts to Orthodoxy—among them Father John, the pastor of this flock, who used to be an Episcopalian.

For the last four-and-a-half years I've been attending the services there while not neglecting my obligations at Saint Rose, my local parish, where I assist at the early Sunday morning Mass and contribute to the fuel collection. My pastor at Saint Rose's, Father Mawn, knows of my double allegiance and wholeheartedly approves. About three years ago Marilyn, the choir director at SaintMary's, invited me to join the bass section. Thus was I initiated into the intricacies of Byzantine chant. It was not as easy as I'd thought; it took nearly two years before I was able to hold my own. Even now it's an adventure when I'm left alone for the bass part. Perhaps it's just a coincidence but I've noticed that Marilyn's hair has become noticeably grayer during this time. I'm a bit like the Swede in McNamara's band, assimilated yet different.

I tried to approach the community of Saint Mary's with discretion and respect and without any sort of agenda or plan, disposed to gratefully receive what they had to offer me and to participate in the measure in which both they and I felt comfortable. Things just sort of happened by themselves, without being forced. I feel as though I've been adopted by the community to the extent that this is possible, given the limits which the canonical situation imposes.

Last year I asked Father John about the possibility of communicating on certain feasts. Since I'd become a fixture at Saint Mary's and one of the most faithful assistants at the liturgies (it's not a big sacrifice for me to cross the street, whereas the majority of the parishioners have a long commute), it seemed to me that this would be "normal." What didn't seem normal was that, after reciting the prayer of Saint John Chrysostom, everyone in this community of which I'd become a part approached the altar while I assured the continuity of the Communion hymn. Father John agreed with the "normality" part but didn't think he had the authority to bypass the canons. It was a good exchange which cleared up a lot of things and left me at peace. The essential of the Eucharist is the love of which it is the symbol, so much so that in Saint John's narrative of the Last Supper the institution of the sacrament is not even mentioned and all the attention is focused on the love of which the sacrament is the sign. For the time being we have to assume the consequences of the collective sins of our churches and it is precisely our mutual fraternal love which can eventually invalidate these consequences.

I don't have any big theological debates with my Orthodox friends; we leave those to the higher-ups. We do, however, freely discuss the good and the bad in our respective churches. It's somewhat ironic, even comical at times. One of the things that most ticks me off in Catholicism is the dictatorial exercise of authority, while the people at Saint Mary's complain about the *lack* of authority and leadership in Orthodoxy, where everyone goes his or her merry way. This is, in fact, the major ecclesiological issue which is separating the two churches, and I can't help but feel that if the *vox populi* (or *consensus fidelium*) on both sides were heard, a creative compromise could be found.

I had been exposed to the Eastern rites in the past. Many aspects of these liturgies struck a deep chord in me: the sense of the transcendence of God, the sensitivity to the presence of the angelic world and the saints of Paradise, the fact of not being afraid to take time for God. But it was only at Saint Mary's that I became immersed in Eastern spirituality. Oddly enough, this led to a rediscovery and revitalization of my own Western traditions, which I came to see in a new light.

The eucharistic mystery presents the same challenge as the Incarnation. Jesus is true God and true man, our beloved brother and *Lord*, an itinerant preacher from Nazareth out of where nothing good could come, who searches his destiny, who becomes weary and afraid, who is considered a screwball by his relatives, and who is one of the Holy Trinity, by whom all things were made, and before whom the Seraphim hide their face. The Eucharist, which prolongs the Incarnation, participates in this duality. According to grace and circumstance we will be moved alternatively by one facet or another of the twofold mystery of our Savior: either by his *kenos* or by the majesty of him who so "humiliates" himself, by his proximity or transcendence. Both should be experienced if we are to approximate the truth, but it is psychologically impossible (I find) to do so simultaneously.

This is also true, I believe, on a collective level. Different cultures have different sensitivities, and even within the same culture, sensitivities may vary according to historical circumstances. This diversity is a collective and mutually complementary testimony—down through the ages and until the day of the Second Coming—of the inexhaustible riches of the Father's gift of the Son in his flesh and in the sacrament of his flesh.

In such a context, no single spirituality or liturgical form can adequately express the manifold aspects of the Incarnation and Eucharist, and this is as it should be. The Word became flesh and Eucharist to be with us until the end of the ages and not as a stranger but as a friend, as he was to his contemporaries. On the banks of Lake Tiberias the Risen Christ prepares a charcoal fire with fish and bread for his awe-struck disciples, tells them to come have breakfast, and serves them, overwhelming their fears by the simplicity of his gestures (John 21:1-14). There is here a familiarity, an "ordinariness" which I find extremely touching, and this is Jesus in his risen state, in the glory of his triumph. The liturgical reforms of Vatican II were meant (at least in part) to remind us of this aspect of the Incarnation.

I think of some of the very simple but intense Eucharists in which I participated years ago in Latin America. They took place in the homes of the poor. With the priest, we prayed and meditated together on the word of God. The eucharistic act took place on a rickety table with no decorations or ornaments. Afterward, a meal was shared among the poor, the crippled, the lame, and the blind—with no questions asked. These were Tiberian Eucharists. They might not have been strictly according to the canons and regulations—even those of post-Vatican II—but I think they were in the spirit of the reforms and they certainly had a deep effect on all of us who took part. The Word became flesh to become accessible to all.

That is one side of the coin, the intuition more typical of the Roman Catholic church. But the familiarity which the reformed liturgy encourages should not lead to trivializing the other pole of the Incarnation. Jesus is not just a "good buddy." He is the Holy Mighty, the Holy Immortal. If Jesus continues to accompany his pilgrim church and is, in this mystical sense, *viator,* a fellow pilgrim, he is, in actuality, in what concerns his human nature, *comprehensor,* glorified at the right hand of the Father. The reality signified by the Eucharist is the exalted and transformed humanity of the Eternal Word; it is the Lamb in his majesty, adored with incense and chants by the twenty-four elders and four living creatures, acclaimed by the myriads of angels and an innumerable white-robed multitude from every race, nation, people, and tongue. It is *this* aspect of the Eucharist which the Eastern liturgies focus upon and of which we should never lose sight. We must never forget *Who* it is who makes himself so near to us.

There is a wonderful complementarity here. What is true of the different liturgies I find also true of the "spiritualities" of the East and the West. The one is marked by a sense of God's transcendent glory, the other by a tenderness toward him who shared and continues to share the misery of our lives, transforming them by his poverty. John Paul II has said on many occasions—and most recently in his apostolic letter *Lumen orientale* where he urges Latin Catholics to open themselves to the treasures of the East—that the church needs to breathe with both its lungs. Personally, I find that incorporating the two liturgies into my life has been a great blessing. This is a grace I would wish for the church as a whole.

January 12, 1996

THE DESCENT INTO HELL

The first time I assisted at the Russian Orthodox Easter Vigil at Saint Mary's in Chelsea, I was disoriented and somewhat disappointed. Everything was "strange," to say the least. There was an emphasis on death, personified as a protagonist of the Paschal drama, as though the liturgy were looking back over its shoulder instead of rejoicing in the Resurrection. The hymnology struck me as extremely naive: Adam and Eve kept popping up, Death was always complaining about being deceived, there were constant references to the tomb and the custom of visiting the graveyards during Easter week. This is not what I am used to. In the Roman liturgy, where the symbolism is much clearer and more logical, we accompany Christ in his Passion and rejoice in his Resurrection as his personal triumph over death. He has been glorified, his integrity restored and magnified, and we, in our turn, hope to share in this victory.

It was the constant references to the Descent into Hell during the Byzantine Paschal liturgy that left me most uncomfortable. Even though this mystery is an article of the Apostles' Creed, the Latin tradition has relegated it to the background—almost as an embarrassment. It is seldom commented upon. When it is, the commentary is usually limited to 1 Peter 3:19 which refers to the preaching of Christ to the spirits in prison. These "spirits" are generally understood as the righteous who died before the coming of Christ and who resided in the "heaven of the patriarchs," a sort of limbo of anticipation. The "preaching" of Christ to the righteous would be the revelation of the redemptive incarnation to them and their subsequent introduction into the beatific vision. For me, the imagery of Christ breaking the gates of hell, leading forth the multitude of the righteous, and trampling death underfoot was related to this very "materialist" conception of the activity of the disembodied soul of Christ among the dead and/or demons.

In an April 6, 1966 article in the *New York Times*, Peter Steinfels opposed the insights of the late Hans Urs von Balthasar to these elaborate scenarios about Christ's descent to the underworld. Von Balthasar relied heavily on the mystical experiences of Adrienne von Speyr for his "Holy Saturday theology." For twenty years, von Speyr relived the Passion during Holy Week. On the afternoon of Good Friday, she would fall into a trance until early Easter Sunday morning and, in this trance-like state, she would experience the descent into hell with Jesus. The disembodied soul of Jesus is in a state of total passivity and solitude, psychologically cut off from others and cut off from God. Hell is the place where God is absent, where there is neither faith nor hope nor love. It is the experience of sin in its essence, of the "second death," the experience of the absence of God and thus of a meaninglessness without light. He who is without sin enters, through obedience, into the absurd. And *because* he is without sin, he experiences the second death in all its horror. This is what it means, in its starkest reality, to assume the sin of the world. According to von Balthasar, in this state of utter dereliction and abandonment during the *triduum mortis,* the knowledge and hope of the Resurrection have lost all meaning, all sense of time has evaporated. The Resurrection will come as an abrupt surprise, as a "bolt of lightning." In such a context, the Eastern imagery depicting the "activity" of Christ in the netherworld appears not only as archaic and infantile but as, quite frankly, misleading. Von Balthasar criticizes it as such.

What von Speyr described and what von Balthasar elaborated on would appear at first glance to be the contrary of what the Byzantine liturgy celebrates. But perhaps not. My own "bolt of lightning" came during my second Holy Week at Saint Mary's. It was an intuition that, in celebrating the Descent into Hell, the Eastern church was tapping into something on another level altogether. This Eastern understanding is concerned not so much with the activity or passivity or psychology of Jesus during the three days his body lay in the tomb, but with the theological implications of the *triduum mortis.* The *descensus ad inferos* represents the *act* of the victory of life over death by the entrance of Life into death, destroying death from within: Where Life has entered, death can no longer exist. He who died on the Cross and entered into death is one of the Holy Trinity, the source of all life. That is why death is truly vanquished and the gates of hell are shattered.

The emphasis here is on the ontological effects of the Paschal mystery, which knows no limits of time or space. For through Jesus, life enters into the kingdom of death and overcomes its terrible darkness. As the Eastern liturgy proclaims, "Adam exults and Eve rejoices" as the bonds of hell are broken. Adam and Eve, representing humanity sitting in darkness and the shadow of death, witness death losing its power over us. God is life, and what happens in his life happens to life itself, to the lives of all. We touch here on the very essence of the redemption: "Death is swallowed up in victory .... O Death where is thy sting?" (1 Cor. 15:54-55).

Other aspects of Jesus' redemptive incarnation—the sacrificial and the propitiatory aspects, and the Resurrection itself—now come into sharper focus, for the physical resurrection of Christ is the effective sign of his triumph over death, and is accomplished during his three days in the tomb, a time that itself now becomes lifegiving. There is absolutely nothing to fear anymore: Death and sin have been vanquished. Even when we enter into the realm of death, we will find Jesus *there*. So powerful and all-embracing is this concept of the triumph over Hades that Origen was led to believe that *nothing* was excluded, that Hades itself was transformed into a paradise and that even the demons were saved.

I have touched here briefly on the fundamental differences of perspective between the mysticisms of Orient and Occident. In Western mysticism, the tendency is to envisage God and his Christ as an objective presence, exterior to us and transcending us. We thus strive to arrive at an intimacy with him. We try to imitate the Christ of the Gospels. We venerate the Blessed Sacrament as an objective presence of Jesus in his glorified state. For the Eastern church, God's presence is experienced as interior: Our relationship with Jesus is that of a shared life, of an indwelling, a divinization, in the Spirit, of our own lives. This is, of course, a question of dominating insights, of emphasis, and not a strict dichotomy.

This difference might account for the diverse manners in which the mystery of the Descent is contemplated in the two traditions. If we consider what happened to God during the *triduum mortis,* the perspective of von Balthasar makes us focus on the death of the Word in all its brutal realism and seriousness. The Latin tradition contemplates with tenderness and awe an event that took place in our history. The Eastern churches focus on the effects of this mystery, what it means for our life, and for our death. As the Easter antiphon repeats, "Christ is risen from the dead, trampling down death by death, and upon those in the tombs bestowing life." This is not just an historical event of the past but an activity taking place among us now. It is as though the Resurrection of Christ were incomplete until it culminates in the resurrection of all in the new heaven and the new earth.

This might also explain why in the Byzantine liturgy the Resurrection is inseparable from the Descent into Hell. The Descent into Hell is the image of our present age. The Resurrection of Christ is the sign and guarantee of the final victory. For nothing is more absurd or contradictory than the entry of Life into death. Yet this is precisely what our faith proposes. The Western church marvels that Life *truly* died, truly suffered death in all its bitterness and disarray. The church of the East rejoices that death is thereby destroyed. And thus, in their mutual complementary testimony, Orthodoxy and Catholicism proclaim the riches of the Paschal mystery and the wonders of the love with which we are loved. How much would each be enriched by listening to the other!

April 11, 1997

A REAL CHURCH LADY

In spring 2003, I finally got to meet Elisabeth Behr-Sigel. At ninety-six, she is the undisputed "grandmother" of Western Christian Orthodoxy and one of its foremost theologians. We had been corresponding for years, yet when she arrived from Paris to deliver a lecture at Boston's Hellenic College, she appeared more frail and diminutive (she is 4' 9") than I had anticipated. Her moral stature is something else, yet her mischievous, self-effacing smile immediately puts you at ease.

Behr-Sigel converted to Orthodoxy when she was twenty-four, but only after she had been one of the first women admitted to advanced theological studies by the Protestant faculty at the University of Strasbourg and the first woman authorized by the Reform Church of Alsace-Lorraine to exercise pastoral ministry.

The Orthodox community which received her—she married an expatriate Russian engineer—was an extraordinary group, composed of immigrants who had been thrown into an entirely foreign culture and context. Freed from the constraints of Russian Orthodoxy's relationship with the state, "Western Orthodoxy" was an idea that began to take shape there.

Behr-Sigel was in the middle of it. She wrote a doctoral thesis on Alexander Bakharev (1822-71), a prophetic figure whose conviction that Orthodoxy should break out of its ghetto mentality cost him his teaching position and led to the proscription of his writings. Behr-Sigel went on to teach at the new Institute of Saint Serge in Paris, and at the Catholic University. Her spiritual father was Lev Gillet (1893-1978), whose major writings appeared under the pseudonym "A Monk of the Eastern Church." She chose that title for her monumental biography of him. With Olivier Clément, she edited, and still edits, *Contacts*, a review that publishes the best of Western Orthodox theology and spirituality. She was also a close friend of Mother Marie Skobstova (1891-1945), whose efforts on behalf of French Jews led to her death in a Nazi concentration camp.

One of Behr-Sigel's major, ongoing efforts has been to reexamine the role of women in Orthodoxy. Without stridency, she requests a soul searching: Why are women not allowed behind the Royal Doors in the sanctuary? When a male child is "churched," why is he brought into the sanctuary, but a female is not? Why were women traditionally considered impure for forty days after childbirth and forbidden to receive the Eucharist? Given such practices, one can imagine the opposition any suggestion that women be allowed to participate in the ministerial priesthood might raise. Yet Behr-Sigel has asked Orthodoxy to consider these issues—and she has been heard. She sees women's rights and egalitarian roles as a cultural phenomenon the church must acknowledge if it is to address the modern world. Nor is the Holy Spirit to be limited by confessional boundaries, she insists. Thus, the ordination of women in other confessions will pose critical ecumenical questions for Orthodoxy, as eucharistic communion among Christians will be definitively compromised if these ordinations are an aberration.

Behr-Sigel's approach to these "hot potato" issues (as she calls them) is consistent with her theology and spirituality. Rather than attack the tradition of the church, she uses what is most venerable and basic in it to bolster her arguments. For example, Orthodox spirituality is centered on the Resurrection, and the great witnesses to this event are Mary of Magdala and the myrrh-bearing women. There is also the theological anthropology of the church fathers, which proclaimed the equality of men and women together as images of God, and the theme of the royal priesthood of all the baptized, who "make" the Eucharist along with the celebrant.

She has also proposed a creative revival of the order of deaconesses that once existed in the Eastern Church. Deaconesses ministered primarily to women, and their role was catechetical and philanthropic. Furthermore, Behr-Sigel urges that the role of priests' spouses in the life of the parish be recognized, dignified, and sacramentalized.

Behr-Sigel is no longer alone in her concerns. In recent years there have been a number of international congresses of Orthodox women to discuss such issues and to make recommendations. Still, her prestige and experience have made her the anchor and natural spokesperson for these groups. While the results have not been spectacular, they are encouraging. Whereas the Catholic Church recently closed the book on any discussion of the ordination of women, Orthodoxy is listening and thinking. In part, that is because of Elisabeth Behr-Sigel. Future generations may well see in her one of the great figures of our time.

January 16, 2004

BACK TO THE FUTURE

Gregory I (pope from 590-604), in a letter to the patriarch of Alexandria, addresses him as his "brother in rank," refuses to be considered "universal pope," and rejects any titles that might "inflate vanity and offend charity." Gregory VII (1073-85), in the text known as *Dictatus papae*, affirms that "only the Roman pontiff can be called universal, use the imperial standards, and allow princes to kiss his feet." At the conclusion of Vatican I (1869-70), when the Greek Catholic patriarch of Antioch, Gregory II Youssef, advanced to kiss the feet of Pius IX, the pope pushed his foot on the patriarch's neck and called him, in substance, a "stubborn mule." During the debates in the council the patriarch had protested that the proposed definitions of papal infallibility were not conformed to tradition—thus provoking the famous response of Pius IX: "I am the tradition!"

In his 1995 encyclical *Ut unum sint*, John Paul II states that he wishes to heed "the request made of me to find a way of exercising the primacy which, while in no way renouncing what is essential to its mission, is none the less open to a new situation." He acknowledges that "for a variety of reasons and against the will of all concerned, what should have been a service sometimes manifested itself in a very different light. I insistently pray the Holy Spirit to shine his light upon us, enlightening all the pastors and theologians of our churches so that we may seek—together, of course—the forms in which this ministry may accomplish a service of love recognized by all concerned."

Let me suggest that those "forms" are already known to us, for they were practiced for much of Christianity's first thousand years. Indeed, the three instances cited in my opening paragraph can be seen to represent three manners of exercising the primacy. "For a whole millennium Christians were united in a brotherly fraternal communion of faith and sacramental life. If disagreements in belief and discipline arose among them, the Roman See acted by common consent as moderator" *(Ut unum sint)*.

It is an undisputed fact that, after the destruction of Jerusalem in A.D. 70, the church of Rome inherited the role of "mother church." Even before the close of the first century, Ignatius of Antioch wrote to the "church in Rome which presides in love." The relationship between Rome and the rest of the Christian world in the first millennium was not always idyllic nor tension-free, but Rome was considered, at least implicitly, as the instrument and sign of ecclesial unity. In the ecumenical councils, the interventions of the bishop of Rome were given special consideration, the arbitration of Rome was sought and respected. However, Rome did not preside "infallibly," at least not in the sense that popes were incapable of error. For example, the Sixth Ecumenical Council (Constantinople III, 680-81) condemned, with the approbation of then Pope Agathon, certain of the Christological positions of Pope Honorius (625-38) as well as those of the late patriarch of Constantinople.

Obviously, the emergence of the papacy as a temporal power brought about a radical change in the way Rome conceived of and exercised its primacy. However justified this assumption of temporal power might be as a "suppliance" in an epoch of chaos and division in the Western world *and* as a guarantee of the political independence of the papacy, it could not but affect the idea Rome had of its spiritual role. In his famous bull *Unam sanctam* (1302), Boniface VIII affirms the absolute temporal power of the pope, his right to judge all other temporal powers and not to be judged by any other. The pope is not just the vicar of Christ; he is his substitute. The bull concludes: "We affirm, declare, and decree that it is absolutely necessary to submit to the Roman pontiff in order to be saved."

The Reformation signaled the decline of the papacy's temporal power, culminating in the humiliation of Pius VI by Napoleon and the plebiscite of 1870, in which the people of Rome, by an overwhelming majority, voted for their incorporation into the new secular Kingdom of Italy. As if to compensate for the loss of political power, the popes of the late nineteenth and early twentieth centuries began to accentuate their spiritual authority. Following Vatican I and its declaration of papal infallibility, *Civiltà Cattolica*, the review of the

Roman Jesuits, serenely declared that "when the pope meditates, it is God who is thinking in him." Don Bosco could affirm, in a text which received the imprimatur, that "Jesus put the pope on the same level as God."

By focusing its ecclesiology on fraternal communion, Vatican II (1962-65) has provided the elements necessary for returning the Christian church to its most venerable traditions. The mystery of the church is realized in the communion of the people of God, a people who has found mercy: "As Christ realized the redemption in poverty and persecution, so is the church called to follow this same road to communicate the fruits of salvation to mankind," the council wrote in its *Dogmatic Constitution on the Church*. "The ministries in the church are at the service of the people of God that all might rejoice in their true Christian dignity and freely attain salvation."

Many years have elapsed since Vatican II, but the consequences of this teaching have yet to permeate the church. It is no easy task to reverse the drift toward papal authoritarianism built up in the course of a millennium. While all sorts of historical, political, and social reasons can be advanced to explain how, as John Paul noted, "what should have been a service sometimes manifested itself in a very different light," there has been a concomitant effort, unconscious perhaps, to justify these deviations by exaggerating certain elements of ecclesiology. In the measure in which the papacy assumed temporal power, it began to see its mission as manifesting the kingship of the triumphant Christ and itself as a sacrament of this kingship. Pushed too far, such a monarchical vision of ecclesial authority has threatened to place the papacy beyond the reach of history itself and individual popes outside the human condition.

Nor has such a mentality been limited to the papacy: it is manifested in the Roman curia in the measure in which it claims to represent a directly inspired papal authority, in the episcopacy insofar as it presumes to possess the truth independently of the faithful. To be sure, the ordained receive a grace of special assistance of the Holy Spirit, but this does not exempt them from the human effort of listening, learning, and searching; if anything, the grace of the sacrament obliges the ordained to *search* the will of God with more diligence and discretion.

Gregory the Great appropriated the magnificent title of "servant of the servants of God." Paul VI was fond of using the same title, and certain of his acts manifested how seriously he took it. John Paul II desired that the papal primacy be at the service of church unity. For this to come about it is crucial that the primacy, all primacy, become a *service* rather than a prerogative, privilege, or power. It is true that "the church is not a democracy," that it has a divinely instituted hierarchical structure. But it is also true that the church is essentially a communion of persons in the Trinitarian life and that this communion cannot be imposed from without. It must surge from within, in freedom and love and in the Holy Spirit. The role of the hierarchy is to provoke, nurture, and promote this communion. Communion cannot be realized without a "reception," a seeking out of the *"sensus fidelium."*

Communion also implies a unity in diversity very different from the uniformity that too often has been exacted in the past. Lip service is given to the respect due to local churches and customs but, in practice, Rome continues to impose its views (for example, in the back and forth over juridical control of American Catholic universities). Yet there is a growing recognition that, in the apostolic tradition, the local church fully manifests the one, holy, catholic, and apostolic church; that it is not just a "part" of the universal church but the plentitude of that church in a given place and assembled around its bishop.

There is no easy answer to the question of how to reunite the Christian churches under the papacy. Still, there seems to be a growing consensus that a starting point would be to return to the situation that existed before the Great Schism of 1054. *Ut unum sint* invokes the church of the first millennium and the role of the Roman See as moderator, by common accord, in cases of disagreement. A return to such simplicity is not inconceivable. It would require, however, rethinking and recasting a thousand years of historical baggage. For one thing, it would mean recognizing that all the councils since the rupture between East and West were not truly ecumenical, but simple synods of the Western church, and thus not universally binding. Paul VI opened the door to such a possibility when, in the solemn commemoration of the seven-hundredth anniversary of the Council of Lyon, recognized by Rome as the fourteenth of the ecumenical councils, he constantly referred to it as the sixth general synod of the Western church. Reunification would require a purification of habits and memories, a shift from a juridical conception of papal authority to a "sacramental" understanding of the papacy as an efficacious sign of church unity recognized and empowered by a common accord.

The sacramental dimension of the primacy cannot be imposed; its authority must be founded on the authority of the truth and not, as has been the case in the past, on the truth of its authority. This is exactly the note that John Paul II hits in *Ut unum sint* when he asks all the pastors and theologians of our churches to seek together with him the forms in which the ministry of Peter may accomplish a service of love *recognized by all*. There is here a confidence that the truth, humbly and prayerfully sought by all concerned, will eventually manifest and impose itself.

Such a willingness to recognize the works of the Holy Spirit in the separated churches and to learn and be enriched by them is already a powerful work of unification. It is Peter *affirming* his brethren and not lording it over them. It would not be contrary to the essential mission of the primacy, for instance, to recognize the jurisdictional autonomy of the Eastern churches and the originality of their traditions. The bishop of Rome would continue to be the patriarch of the West, exercising immediate jurisdiction according to Western customs and only intervening outside of this jurisdiction as a moderator when there are "disagreements in belief and discipline." Perhaps a similar rapport could be established with the Reformed churches, whereby their structures, traditions, and charisms would be respected while enriching them with the graces of communion with the universal church.

Of course, an unwillingness to pursue seriously the possibility of unity is not the failure of Rome alone. Far from it. It is no secret that there has been a resurgence of conservatism and parochialism in many of the Christian churches. But whatever might be the difficulties, it is asked of the Christian churches to *tend towards* an ideal of unity. This ideal may seem utopian, but that should not deter us.

January 15, 1999

O ne way to move beyond the current stalemate in our efforts toward Christian unity is to take the state of the undivided church, before 1054, as a point of reference. The Vatican II decree on ecumenism states as much and John Paul II, in his 1995 encyclical, *Ut unum sint,* recalls that "for a whole millennium Christians were united in a brotherly, fraternal communion of faith and sacramental life. If disagreements in belief and discipline rose among them, the Roman See acted by common consent as mediator." And there is a broader consensus. The recent attempt at reunification between the Catholic Melkite and the Orthodox in the Antiochean church took their common heritage as the basis of a projected merger. Most of the Reformed churches would accept the teachings of the ecumenical councils of the first millennium. The ongoing Catholic dialogue with the "Oriental churches" (Armenian, Syrian, etc.), communities that did not accept the teachings of the Council of Chalcedon, is leading to the conclusion that it was misunderstanding, rather than doctrinal divergences, that caused the rupture. In short, using the church of the first millennium as a model is our best hope for ecumenical progress.

Imagine a future, truly ecumenical council where all the parties who profess the Nicean Creed—the Roman church, those who issued from the Protestant Reformation (Lutheran, Anglican, etc.), the Orthodox, and Oriental Christians—sit down as equals, without arrogance or sense of superiority, and analyze their respective histories since the rupture. Each would try to see the positive in what the Holy Spirit has accomplished in other churches and how the particular grace of each might enrich all. The goal of the council would be for the churches to pass from coexistence to what might be called "pro-existence": existing for the other and not just alongside one another. This would require a profound conversion and purification of memories.

If this were to be done, the churches might well discover that their particular charisms and insights are more complementary than antagonistic, that there is more paradox than "clarity" in the Christian mysteries, and even that differences are necessary if certain elements of the truth are to be manifested.

In *Crossing the Threshold of Hope,* John Paul II said: "Why has the Holy Spirit permitted all these divisions?... Could it not be that the divisions have also been a path continually leading the church to discover the untold wealth contained in Christ's gospel?...It is necessary for humanity to achieve unity through plurality to learn to come together in one church even while presenting a plurality of ways of thinking and acting of civilizations and cultures."

If the starting point for our hypothetical council is to be the state of the undivided church before 1054, this would imply, for the Roman church, the recognition that all its councils since the rupture have not been truly ecumenical. In other words, they have been local councils of the Western church and not universally binding. Paul VI opened the door to such a possibility when, at the seven hundredth anniversary of the Council of Lyon, he referred to it as "the sixth of the general synods held in the West." This does not mean that the teachings of these Western councils or the papal "dogmatic" definitions would cease to oblige Roman Catholics, nor does it imply that other Christians should not take them very seriously. Often, teachings and dogmas develop from polemical situations and are affirmations of an aspect of the truth believed to be compromised or neglected. Christianity is a religion of paradoxes, where we are often asked to affirm, as absolutes, terms that are apparently contradictory. How to reconcile free will with the omniscience of God, the reality of history with the eternal instant, justice with mercy, the true divinity and true humanity of Jesus? We can only seize and articulate one of these terms at a time. Might this not be the profound theological reason for so many divisions? By taking one side of the paradox and affirming it absolutely we apparently negate the other side. That's when anathemas begin to fly and dialogue becomes impossible.

In reaching common ground it is necessary to evaluate the true significance of a particular teaching, taking into consideration the circumstances in which it developed. The definition of papal infallibility is a case in point. One of the complexities of the historical situation surrounding Vatican I was the ambition of European secular rulers to control national episcopacies. Given this papal concern, it is remarkable to read the explanation of the proposed dogma as it was presented to the council by Monsignor Vinzenz Gasser, the official "relator." According to Gasser's presentation, "the most appropriate situation for the exercise of infallibility would be when scandals concerning the faith, dissensions, and heresies come to pass in a given church and they are of such a magnitude that the bishops of that church (individually or in provincial council) cannot cope with them and, for this reason, feel obliged to submit them to the Holy See." Moreover, infallibility is linked to the mission of the pope to "conserve the church in the unity of faith and charity and restore this unity when it is disturbed."

What Gasser is describing here is, in fact, the practice of the undivided church of the first millennium. The pope is the ultimate judge in matters of controversy regarding the faith which cannot be resolved on a local level The definition of infallibility does not separate the pope from the church, since he can only exercise this prerogative insofar as he is recognized as the efficacious sacrament of the unity of the church. The church is not infallible because of the pope; the pope is infallible because of the church. The famous *"ex sese, non ex consensu ecclesiae"* (the pope is infallible by reason of his office, not through the consent of the church) has its justification in the vagueness of the "consent of the church."

If it be accepted that Vatican I was a local council of the Western church, the declaration that "the bishop of Rome possesses a true episcopal power of jurisdiction, ordinary and immediate, over the totality of the pastors and faithful" would maintain its validity for the Western church. Outside of the jurisdiction of the Western patriarch, Rome would cede to local customs. As Cardinal Joseph Ratzinger himself declared, "Rome should not apply the doctrine of Roman primacy of Vatican I to the East because this 'dogma' was formulated and practiced after the separation of 1054: it can only oblige the East to maintain what was practiced during the first millennium."

In *Ut unum sint,* John Paul II recognizes the need to revise the mechanisms of papal authority and asks for help to bring about this revision. A truly ecumenical council would help the Catholic church to distinguish the essential role of Rome as the "mother church" (after the fall of Jerusalem) vis-à-vis the rest of the Christian world. But the jurisdictional structure Rome has given itself in the second millennium need not be imposed on the other churches. The Reform bodies, for example, have elaborated their own structures, many of which are often more conformed to the primitive traditions of collegiality and charisms. Similarly, the ecclesial intuitions of the Eastern and Reformed churches could become a very profitable complement to the Roman vision.

But what about the Marian "dogmas"? The Immaculate Conception and the Assumption are rooted in the patristic axiom that Mary was the *worthy* Mother of God, a worthy tabernacle of the Most High. But she was also the daughter of Abraham, the heiress of the faith of the patriarchs and prophets. The faith of the Virgin is the culmination of a whole history of humanity's response to the revealing acts of God and the experience of his redemptive love. The extraordinary graces given to Mary in view of her role in redemption do not put her outside of salvation history or make her any less our sister. In his magnificent epilogue to the *Sign of Jonas,* Thomas Merton has God speaking: "What is vile has become precious. What is now precious was never vile; for what is vile I know not at all." Baptism accomplishes in us what the Immaculate Conception accomplished in Mary. We become, as it were, immaculately conceived—and the power of his grace will eventually transform our earthly bodies. There is nothing here, as far as I can see, which does not correspond to the perennial faith of the undivided church.

What is objectionable is the fact that these "dogmas" were proclaimed unilaterally by the Roman church. What are also objectionable are certain forms of Marian piety that so exalt the Mother of God that they distance her from us and the vicissitudes of the human condition.

What of the churches separated from Rome? Orthodoxy, during the last millennium, has continued to probe the mysteries of faith. Gregory of Palmas expounded on the implications of our participation in the divine life; the theology of the "divine energies" took form; and ecclesiology evolved with the concept of *sobornost* ("conciliarity"). Amid persecution and humiliation, a profound mystical theology was born, a pearl of great price for the universal church.

The Reformation, on the other hand, brought into focus the royal priesthood of the laity and their immense dignity. The notion of the sacraments as gifts was an important contribution which had hitherto been neglected. The Pentecostal movement, for its part, returned the Holy Spirit to its rightful place in the lives of the faithful. There are those churches which have highlighted the mission of evangelizing the poor, others which have focused on the exigencies of fraternal charity and the common life. An attitude of "pro-existence" would assume all that is positive in the evolution of Christianity in its diverse forms. It will require of all Christians a great humility and openness to the Holy Spirit to be able to put things in their proper perspective, to distinguish what is essential and authentic and what are the vicissitudes of a sinful history. The reformers reacted against the clerical abuse of power, and rightly so. But was this sufficient grounds for rejecting the sacramental structure of the church's hierarchy and the ancient tradition of apostolic succession? The apostolic power, as Saint Paul describes it, is rooted and exercised in human weakness, fragility, and humiliation, but it is a divine power nonetheless. The Reformed churches would need to reconsider their rejection of apostolic succession, as Catholicism and Orthodoxy would need to reconsider the essential nature and exercise of this "power."

It would be fitting that the church of Rome seek to convoke our hypothetical "pro-existence" council but it need not be so. In fact, it might be preferable if the initiative came from Orthodoxy or the World Council of Churches. There will no doubt be elements in each church adamantly opposed to any "compromise." The general reception and even anger that greeted the Congregation for the Doctrine of the Faith's 2000 document *Dominus Jesus* was highly significant. The reaction to its tone, timing, and content, both within the Roman church and without, was a striking example of the *sensus fidei* at work, refusing to recognize what is not of the Spirit. Still, it must be remembered that the truly ecumenical councils of the first millennium produced great and charismatic saints to guide the church. There is no reason to believe that the Holy Spirit is any less capable of raising up mighty saints today.

January 12, 2001

ORTHODOXY AND DISSENT

St. Pius X, in his encyclical *Vehementer* (1902), wrote: "By its very nature the church is a society of unequals; it is composed of two categories of persons: the pastors and the flocks. Only the hierarchy moves and directs...the duty of the flock is to let itself be governed and submissively carry out the orders of those who direct them." Such a simplistic understanding of the church would seem to have been supplanted by the declarations of Vatican II, as well as by the social and cultural changes that have taken place in the century since *Vehementer*'s promulgation.

When it comes to the church's teachings about sexual morality, however, this clericalist view is still very much with us. Some still believe that everything the church has ever taught about sex is universal, timeless, rooted in the very nature of things. On this view, once these moral teachings are questioned, their dogmatic foundation is weakened, and everything falls apart. Any bishop who wants to remain in good grace with the Vatican is obliged to uphold these teachings in his pastoral directives. For others, the church's moral teachings are unreasonable, anachronistic, even hypocritical. In their view, Catholic sexual morality should adapt to important changes in contemporary culture. There is a swelling discontent among the laity with an ecclesiastical authority already compromised by the sexual-abuse scandal. Such radical differences of perspective have turned the church into a battlefield where the opposing troops hurl anathemas at one another from their trenches.

It hasn't always been the moral rigor of the church's teachings that provoked dissent. In other periods of the church's history, dissent arose in reaction to a perceived laxity on the part of church authorities. Bishops were accused of watering down Christian moral obligations and tolerating pagan adulterations of the gospel. In fact, most of the great heresies originated as criticisms of the church's excessive tolerance—from the Donatists, who opposed the reception of lapsed Christians back into the church, to the

Cathars, who aspired to an unrealistic purity, to Reformers who began by opposing indulgences and ended up rejecting the sacramental channels of grace. Such rigoristic dissent sometimes spurred reform and purification within the church, but too often it occasioned schisms and aberrations of zeal that could have been avoided had there been a minimum of humility on both sides. In the past, as in the present, dissent led to a hardening of positions with unintended consequences.

To understand dissent, you first have to understand authority. Authority in the church must be based on truth. Episcopal authority is not the *source* of truth, as some would have us believe. "What is truth?" The question posed by Pilate was left unanswered by Truth Himself who stood before him, humiliated, in the praetorium. We too humiliate Truth when we abase it to our level and pretend to have power over it. Truth is a divine name and to pretend to possess it, individually or collectively, is to manufacture an idol. We can no more claim to possess truth than we can claim to possess justice. And this holds for the church's pastors, as well as for their flock.

For Christians, truth is Someone who possesses *us*, Someone who reveals as much of Himself to us as we can bear. It is this self-revealing Truth who founds authority in the church. The role of the magisterium is to maintain the purity of revelation by warning against aberrations without denying or minimizing the elements of truth behind them. The magisterium might be infallible in what it affirms, yet what it affirms is often just one aspect of a complex reality whose components are still not fully understood. In pulling out the weeds, there is the danger of uprooting the good grain, and this has often happened in the past. Examples abound. In the wake of the Enlightenment, as Rome felt threatened by anticlericalism and feared the disappearance of social structures that were supposed to reflect God's will, popes condemned democracy and liberty of conscience. The church, individually and collectively, is forever *docens et discens*, teaching and learning. To deny the possibility of further elucidation of doctrine is blasphemous. It is tantamount to pronouncing the church dead, no longer vivified by the Spirit nor tending toward an ultimate manifestation still to come, when all that has been hidden will be revealed. The reception and assimilation of God's word by the pilgrim church will forever be partial and variable. It will depend partly on psychological, social, and historical circumstances. Every cultural cycle, every scientific advance, can serve to deepen our understanding of revelation, to illuminate one or another of its aspects. There is, however, an objective deposit of faith, constantly elucidated through the ages, to which the blood of martyrs has borne witness. Any development in the church is made possible only by what has preceded it, yet the intoxication of a novelty often leads to a rejection of what went before.

Dissent can be a sign of vitality; it can draw out the latent riches of revelation. The scribe versed in the affairs of the Kingdom will continually bring forth old things and new. Rather than automatically suppressing it, therefore, the magisterium should treat it with cautious respect, remembering that the Spirit is still at work, and the church still a work in progress. Rigidity and narrowness of vision can lead to the sin against the Spirit—and this sin can be a collective one.

Today, the most acute problems of dissent usually have to do with the church's moral teachings. Traditional Catholic moral theology generally abstracts from concrete historical and social contexts and considers not particular men and women, but "human nature" faced with hypothetically clear-cut options. Human nature, however, does not exist apart from real human beings, who must act in situations full of ambiguity. Very often we find ourselves in "damned if you do, damned if you don't" situations, where even the best option may not seem to be a good one. Pastoral common sense usually (but not always!) takes this complexity into consideration, but the official teachings of the church continue to define good and evil in terms of black and white, with little nuance or compassion, thus alienating many from the sacramental sources of grace.

Of course, the church must maintain the sublimity of the Christian vocation, which surpasses our ordinary human capabilities. Were the church to reduce the exigencies of sanctity to what is supposed to be realistic, it would betray its mission: "Be perfect as your Heavenly Father is perfect." St. Thomas tells us that we fulfill this precept by *tending toward* perfection. Weighed down by individual and collective sin, faced with the complexities and ambiguities of ordinary experience, we can only tend toward perfection in a very imperfect way. Moreover, the emphasis on this or that aspect of the moral teachings of the church tends to shift from one time and place to another, and an exaggerated stress on one set of moral values often leads to the neglect of others equally important. Here, too, there is room for legitimate dissent. The conflicts that take place in the human heart are seldom as simple as the church's official teachings would have us believe. The problem isn't so much what the church proclaims as *how* it proclaims the truths of the faith and applies them to concrete situations. We are asked to *think* with the church (*sentire cum ecclesia*), but it is equally important for us to *love* as the church has been called to love. For the church is *mater* as well as *magistra*, and a mother listens compassionately to her children. Thinking or loving, the church's model is Christ, who imposed himself on no one and took upon himself the sins of all.

What is especially disconcerting is that those who speak in the name of the church have often excused the church's past sins and errors by invoking considerations—historical conditions, the lack of a good alternative—denied to individual Christians living now. Is there not a double standard here? The "dispensers of light" are as much in need of mercy as their flocks are.

The safekeeping of the deposit of faith and the upholding of the Christian moral code are confided to the church's hierarchy. The bishops are not, however, the exclusive owners of the spirit of discernment. Historically, this gift has often been manifest in the little ones of God, in the "sensus fidelium." It is precisely this charisma that stimulates the church's growth in wisdom and in grace. There is a necessary tension between the function of the hierarchy and the prophetic instinct of the people of God. That tension could and should be fruitful, but in reality it is often bitter and sterile. It might well be that the prophetic élan in the church is especially at work in the poor and the unrecognized, in the little ones to whom is revealed what is hidden from the wise and mighty. One of the great contributions of liberation theology has been to remind the church of the privileged place of the poor in the Kingdom of God.

It might be well to remember that, during a period of great confusion following the Council of Nicaea in the fourth century, imperial decrees, confirmed by local councils of bishops, imposed Arian beliefs. According to St. Jerome "nearly all the churches in the whole world, under the presence of peace and the emperor, are polluted with the communion of the Arians." Even Pope Liberius, bowing to pressure from the emperor, communicated with the Arians and excommunicated the defenders of Nicaea. The faith professed at Nicaea was conserved by the laity and parish priests, while the great majority of the hierarchs maneuvered, quibbled, and compromised.

It is not enough for the church's hierarchy to praise the fidelity of lay Catholics; it must also be willing to learn from them. And that requires bishops to acknowledge humbly that they don't yet know everything about the will of God—that it is still revealing itself to us, and sometimes surprising us. The bishops, like their flocks, are still pilgrims on the way. Like the rest of us, they should be looking for signs ahead.

February 8, 2013

THE LORD DELIGHTS

"When one tries to speak lovingly of God, all human words become like the tears of blind lions seeking sources in the desert."
—Léon Bloy

Not long ago I discovered the work of Daniel Bourguet, a Lutheran minister who lives as a hermit in the south of France. The first books of his I read were adapted from retreats he had given during Lent and Passiontide. Bourguet's pious style might put some people off—it is a style better suited to oral presentation than to the page—but if one can look past it to the substance of his reflections, one will find some remarkable insights. I was so impressed by his work that I translated one of his books into English and naïvely set out to find a publisher. I never found one. I shared my translation with several friends, hoping for some encouragement and also wanting to share what I thought was a gold mine. Nobody seemed particularly impressed. What I found to be quite moving was considered too mystical or sentimental.

In retrospect, I think the problem may have been Bourguet's strange insistence that God has "sentiments," that he feels our pain and rejoices when we turn toward him. Many of us consider this way of talking about God to be childish. Yet in the Bible God reveals himself as having very human emotions—even some that are not very pretty, like anger and jealousy. God is described as changing his mind and repenting of evils he has allowed. In the creation narrative, we are told that God made man in his image and likeness. This means that we are in some way like God, but it also means that God is in some way like us. This is the basic relationship on which revelation and, ultimately, the Incarnation are based. Theology tells us that all our discourse about God is analogical. God speaks to us about himself truly, but in a language we can understand. The divine reality exceeds that language: it is unimaginable, unspeakable. The challenge is to acknowledge the similarity between us and God without forgetting the radical dissimilarity. We are always in danger of drifting toward either anthropomorphism or agnosticism. I worry that the tendency within Christianity today is toward a kind of agnosticism, in which God is relegated to some unknowable sphere and religion is reduced to a kind of moralism—to actions rather than words.

This is understandable, since the culture at large has become more and more agnostic. More and more people are describing themselves as "none of the above" in surveys of religious affiliation. "Spirituality" is in, and dogma is out. We are part of that larger culture and we need to engage with it, to accept what is authentic in its insights. No doubt there was an overemphasis on dogma in the past, and so now there is a reaction against it. On another level, there has also been a reaction against a very sentimental and basically egoistical type of piety, which neglected the social imperatives of our faith.

Still, I think we should be careful about overcompensating. There is another point of view that we are in danger of forgetting— God's own point of view. We can grasp something of that point of view by what God tells us about himself in the scriptures, but also by what he leaves to our imagination. There is, for example, the perennial problem of suffering in God. Theological wisdom tells us that God is impassible, almighty, perfectly happy. But we cannot really imagine an indifferent and impassive and happy God serenely watching his creatures destroy themselves. The whole mystery of the Incarnation says something entirely different. One of the themes Bourguet develops is that of the apparent silence of the Father during the Passion of the Son. The Father sends his Son a comforting angel during his crisis in the garden of Gethsemane. And there is the mysterious apparition of Simon of Cyrene, who is identified as the father of Alexander and Rufus. In fact, Simon is the only biblical personage who is identified not by his father but by his sons. We are to think of him, then, as a father, and perhaps as a figure of the Father of Jesus, helping him bear his cross. Again, we see the Father expressing his immense sorrow in the tearing apart of the curtain of the Holy of Holies; it is as if he were tearing his vestments in grief. From these discreet signs, we can sense something of a silent suffering too great for words.

Can we speak of God's happiness, his beatitude, as something actually "happening" in God, despite the fact that, according to classical theology, he is beyond all change? Can we not see the human reactions of Jesus as reflecting the sentiments of God? "He who sees me, has seen the Father." Have we become too sophisticated to believe that we can make God happy or sad, to take scripture at its word—at God's word—when it tells us that the Lord delights in and rejoices over us (Zepheniah 3:17)? One of the best sermons I ever heard was on why we should pray. The preacher's answer: because God likes us to pray to him. End of sermon.

September 9, 2016

A DESECRATED LAND

The Mount of Olives, like every piece of real estate in or near Jerusalem, particularly the walled-in Old City, is layered with historical, political, and theological significance. The Mount, situated to the northeast across the Kidron Valley, rises several hundred feet above the Old City, the biblical Mount Zion, and is within easy walking distance. From there, the view of the valley and of Jerusalem is panoramic and evocative. It takes in not only modern Jerusalem, with its hotels and high rises, but the Old City's medieval walls, mosques, churches, and what remains of the fabled Temple.

An enormous Jewish cemetery, ancient but still used, spreads over most of the southern slope and into the valley. It looks like an ugly gash, slashed out of the otherwise placid brown landscape. Here, among an estimated one hundred fifty thousand graves, are said to be the tombs of the prophets Hosea, Zechariah, and Malachi, and of King David's renegade son, Absalom. Jewish tradition has it that on the last day, when full justice is revealed, the resurrection of the dead will commence here (the symbolic Valley of Jehoshaphat), to be inaugurated by the prophet Ezekiel sounding the shofar. With the covenant fulfilled, the face of the earth will be renewed.

According to the prophecy of Zechariah, the Mount will be split in two, from east to west, signifying the final return of Yahweh and all his saints, and the Holy City will be transformed. In the vision of Ezekiel, it was on the Mount of Olives that the Glory of God rested when it departed the Temple. When the Glory returns (Zech. 14:8), all the peoples will come to the purified city to celebrate the Feast of Tabernacles and to give God praise.

After the Arab conquest of 637, the Mount of Olives became the center of Jewish worship for those Jews still allowed to remain in Jerusalem. The most poignant of all Mount of Olives rituals was the lamentation over the destruction of the Temple, the Holy of Holies—its ruins in full view across the valley, desecrated and expropriated.

At the base of the Mount of Olives today is the Orthodox church of the Dormition of the Virgin; silent and dark, buried in a cave, it is discreet and prayerful. A little farther south is the more modern Basilica of the Nations, the traditional site of Gethsemane. A half-dozen ancient olive trees in the patio of the basilica are treated as witnesses to the night of Jesus' agony. Further up the mount is a magnificent Russian monastery in the extravagant Muscovite style, its onion domes glistening. Beyond that, about halfway up the mount, is the Franciscan church of Dominus Flevit (The Lord Wept), with a stirring view of Mount Zion and the ancient city. Higher still and across the way is the Church of the Pater Noster, with the Lord's Prayer reproduced in a variety of languages—many I had never heard of. Near the summit is a more recent construction, a Mormon university where concerts are offered periodically. On the summit itself, an ancient church that once marked the site of Jesus' Ascension is now a mosque. A newer Church of the Ascension constructed by German Lutherans, a hotel, and some Catholic religious houses are nearby. Seen in season from Mount Zion across the valley, this part of the mount appears orderly, green, and almost rural. In Jewish tradition, the olive branch the dove brought Noah after the flood came from here.

In contrast, there is practically no vegetation on the southern slope where the cemetery lies. The sun beats down mercilessly on the trash and the dirt, rocks, and toppled tombstones that litter the place. The locals say it has been a burial ground forever, the cemetery of Jerusalem, desecrated a thousand times over. Prior to Israel's victory in the 1967 war, Jordanians reportedly used the tombstones for military construction and for latrines.

The cemetery is the sole Jewish presence immediately discernible on the mountain today, and it seems a somewhat humiliated one. The city that looked down on it from above, to which the tribes of Israel went up rejoicing, was razed by the Romans. Today it is surrounded by Turkish walls and crowned with churches, mosques, and the glistening dome of the Muslims' Noble Sanctuary. Only the city's ancient Jewish Quarter and the Wailing Wall link it unmistakably to its Davidic past.

Standing in the valley, I can't but wonder how a pious Jew feels as he or she gazes on this violated graveyard, veritably screaming for the resurrection of the dead. Is there any consolation in the fact that the Christian and Muslim intruders consider themselves, in their own way, descendants of Abraham? That they would not have existed had it not been for the promises made to their father in the faith? That even for them, salvation comes from the Jews? Does that offer reassurance?

The humiliation of the Cenacle, located across the Kidron on Mount Zion itself, is more discreet. The traditional site of the Last Supper, of Jesus' post-Resurrection appearance in the upper room, and of the descent of the Holy Spirit at Pentecost, is honored by some Jews as the burial place of King David. Unlike most Christian sites in the Old City, the historicity of the Cenacle is fairly well attested to. Bishop Epiphanius (310-403), a native of Palestine, relying on second-century documents, stated that "Hadrian...found the city entirely razed to the ground and the Temple destroyed and trampled upon with the exception of some houses and a certain small church of the Christians which had been constructed in that place in which the disciples, after the Savior was taken up into heaven from the Mount of Olives, betaking themselves, mounted to the Cenacle."

The early Christian community that had taken refuge in Pella, a city of the Decapolis beyond the northern border of Israel, in AD 66 (before the first Jewish revolt against the Romans) would certainly have returned to the place from which the first community had arisen, and which was the traditional "seat" of St. James, the first "bishop" of Jerusalem. As the site of the institution of the Eucharist and also the descent of the Holy Spirit, the Cenacle would be the mother of all Christian churches. In fact, a church built around the Cenacle came to be called simply the Church on Mount Zion. Somehow, the Cenacle seems to have physically survived the vicissitudes of the many occupations. The Crusaders discovered a two-story chapel there in which an upper room was associated with the events of

Pentecost and the lower room with the washing of the feet and the appearance of the risen Christ. The church was destroyed, but the upper room still stands.

The fate of the lower room seems truly bizarre. It is said that around 1167, following the collapse of a wall, some tombs, richly decorated, were found and identified as those of David and Solomon. This claim seems dubious, because more ancient sources locate David's tomb elsewhere. In fact, the site is commonly called "the false tomb of King David." Still, the Crusaders erected a cenotaph there. Today, it is covered with a velvet cloth embroidered with verses from the psalms. Since Muslims also venerate the memory of David, the Turks eventually declared the place a Muslim sanctuary. In 1523, that status was extended to the upper room and access to it was forbidden to Christians.

Today, each space has its separate entrance. Jews and Christians are now admitted to the lower room, which is dominated by the cenotaph surrounded by candles. The impression is that of a closed-casket wake in progress. This lower room has an intriguing niche that, in a synagogue, would normally be the place where the Torah is kept. But instead of facing the site of the Temple, as would be customary, the niche looks toward the Church of the Holy Sepulchre. This has been taken as an indication that the room was used by a Judeo-Christian community in Jerusalem.

The upper room remains divided in two: the room of the Last Supper and the ancient chapel of the Holy Spirit. When I visited several years ago, the chapel of the Holy Spirit was closed. It is normally considered off-limits to non-Muslims, though it is not an active mosque. What can be seen, the room of the Last Supper, is an empty space with Arabic motifs on its columns and walls. Here a niche indicates the direction of Mecca. For centuries Christians were barred from the Cenacle except on Holy Thursday and Pentecost, when Franciscan friars were allowed to pray there on the condition that no liturgy be celebrated. It was only at the end of the last century that the upper room was partially reopened for Christians to visit. When Pope John Paul II made his pilgrimage to the Holy Land in

2000, he was allowed to celebrate the Eucharist in the upper room—the first and only time in more than four hundred years.

Although the Jewish cemetery in the valley below has been desecrated repeatedly, the Cenacle has been demeaned almost by default. Visitors can't get in to see the whole thing, and what they are allowed to view seems a dilapidated room that could be found almost anywhere in the ancient Middle East. Still, for Christians, this is the place where the church was born. To me, the despoliation of the Kidron cemetery and the emptiness of the Cenacle proclaim not only the powerlessness of God, but a love that prefers humiliation to imposition. Out of the silence of ruins, God's voice can be heard in a remarkable way.

Aquinas, in his commentary on the Beatitudes, contemplates Jesus washing the feet of his disciples—and is amazed. It is as if God were making of us his gods, and his vulnerability is a scandal. In curious and sad ways, the Cenacle and the cemetery beneath the Mount of Olive seem to make a mockery of God's promises. Both challenge us, at the levels of faith and hope, to believe and trust in a God whose name cannot be uttered.

As I gazed around the Cenacle, disappointed and not knowing what to think, I noticed a pigeon in the niche that indicates the direction of Mecca. It was only much later that I thought to ask what the difference is between a pigeon and a dove. I was told that both are of the same family—and are hardly distinguishable.

March 24, 2006

A CHRISTIAN AND THE QUR'AN

In early 2009, the Ministry of Culture of the Islamic Republic of Iran awarded its World Prize for the Book of the Year to *The Banquet: A Reading of the Fifth Sura of the Qur'an*—originally published in French as *Le Festin: Une lecture de la sorate al-Mâ'ida.* The book's author was invited to Tehran to receive the award from President Mahmoud Ahmadinejad, and was subsequently asked to present his findings to academic gatherings in Tehran and at Iran's principal Shiite university at Qum. He managed to win over his initially skeptical audience and was invited to give a lecture to seminary students (which his travel plans did not permit).

The irony in all this is that the author, Michael Cuypers, is a Belgian Catholic, a member of the Little Brothers of Jesus who had been expelled from Iran in 1989. He had initially lived in Tabriz at a leper colony run by the brothers but was later asked by his order to start a foundation in Tehran. There he studied Farsi and Iranian culture at Tehran University. But when some Iranian students were expelled from Belgium, the Iranian government retaliated by expelling two Belgian citizens, one of whom was Cuypers. He then moved to Egypt, where he learned Arabic and got a job as a file clerk at the Institute of Oriental Studies, run by the Dominicans. When the director of the Institute learned that Cuypers had a gift for analyzing texts, he asked Cuypers to apply his skills to the Qur'an. A religious brother who had wanted nothing more than to live with the poor had become a scholar, almost by accident.

Around the same time, Cuypers was introduced to the work of Roland Meynet, SJ, a specialist in analyzing rhetorical structures in the Bible. Cuypers sent Meynet a copy of an article in which he analyzed several *suras* of the Qur'an. He felt that the same Semitic mentality at work in the Bible could be found in the composition of the Qur'an.

The method Meynet applies to the Bible and Cuypers to the Qur'an is quite different from standard historical criticism. It takes the sacred texts as written but attempts to understand the underlying structures (the "rhetorical composition") that unite the seemingly disparate parts of a text. The premise is that a logic very different from that of the Greeks and Romans is at work, and that understanding this distinctive logic is key to unlocking the texts.

At first sight, the Qur'an reads like a series of fragments, presented with little apparent structure—something akin to literary stream of consciousness. Of course, the same can be said of certain biblical books. The prophets, for example, often announce, seemingly in the same breath, both the most tragic destinies and exalted promises of glory. In the Torah, the most banal—and even shocking—ritual prescriptions sit alongside sublime calls for social justice and love of God and neighbor, as though all were on the same plane. Meynet affirmed that these biblical juxtapositions were indeed coherent, but that they play on a different register, one we need to rediscover. Cuypers affirmed the same of the Qur'an, shedding new light on its subtle intricacies, beauty, and coherence (some Muslim scholars pointed out that these attributes are hardly surprising to those who believe that the words of the Qur'an are those of Allah to his Prophet). The techniques and technicalities of Cuypers's method are complicated and can be disconcerting, at least initially, to the Western mind. But his conclusions are enlightening.

Beginning in the nineteenth century, non-Muslim scholars in the West applied various techniques from modern science (historical and literary criticism, linguistics, etc.) to their study of the Qur'an. Those attempts were usually spurned by Muslims, because of their novelty, but also because of their polemical overtones. In contrast, Cuypers applies his method prudently and respectfully. In his award-winning book, he concentrates on a single *sura* that has puzzled Islamic scholars for centuries and given rise to a multiplicity of interpretations.

Muslim scholars are accustomed to analyzing the Qur'an verse by verse, without considering the immediate literary context or analyzing the interconnections of the verses. To resolve apparent contradictions in the Qur'an, commentators traditionally have recourse to a Qur'anic verse in which God states that he abrogates a law only in order to give a more perfect one. This understanding led commentators to give preference to apparently more restrictive laws over seemingly more moderate ones. But in his study, Cuypers demonstrates that the verse in question refers to the Mosaic Law, not to Qur'anic Law.

The Fifth Sura concerns, among other things, the relationship among Muslims, Jews, and Christians. It refers often to the covenant described in Deuteronomy and Numbers, and it concludes with an invitation by Jesus to a heavenly banquet. At times, the *sura* refers to "peoples of the book" (Christians and Jews) as enemies of Islam. In other sections, this hostility seems to apply only to those who have not followed the teachings given by Moses, the prophets, and Jesus. For historical reasons, the verses that nourish Muslim identity and forbid alliances with Jews and Christians are considered definitive. Cuypers shows that the symmetry of the text puts the emphasis on the universal values of Islam. The enigmatic banquet scene where Jesus asks for "a banquet table from heaven to be a feast for the first among us and the last among us" (Sura 5,114) corresponds textually to an earlier segment of the same *sura* (5,3) where Allah declares, "Today I have completed your religion for you and I have perfected my blessing upon you." The two verses, which appear at the end and at the beginning of the chapter, are symmetrical and "foundational." Even though Christians are encouraged to enter the Islamic covenant, religions are destined to coexist. Using his "rhetorical method," Cuypers explains that one of the intended meanings of the chapter is that God permitted four religions (Islam, Judaism, Gnosticism, and Christianity). Had he wished to do so, God "would have made a single community from them," but in his unfathomable wisdom he did otherwise, so that "they might surpass one another in good actions," and thus challenge one another to better live God's teachings (5,48).

Cuypers's award, which passed under the radar of the Western media, is significant—and perhaps prophetic. That the Iranian clerical establishment not only listened to Cuypers but was willing to learn from him challenges our stereotypes of Iran—and of the Muslim world in general. Still, the award does not necessarily constitute a breakthrough in Muslim-Christian relations. Islam, after all, incorporates a multitude of different and sometimes antagonistic tendencies; to some Muslims, Tehran's gesture might seem to border on blasphemy. Nonetheless, the prize does indicate vitality and openness in Iranian intellectual life, and this points to the possibility of dialogue in the future. After all, it was contact with Islam and its sense of the absolute holiness of God, its sense of community, and its self-dispossessing hospitality that led Christians like Louis Massignon and Charles de Foucauld to a greater appreciation of those values in their own tradition.

In *Crossing the Threshold of Hope*, Pope John Paul II said this about differences among Christians:

> Why did the Holy Spirit permit such divisions?... There can be two answers to this question: a *negative* response—these divisions are the result of peoples' sins; the other response is more *positive*. Might not these divisions be a way that has led and continues to lead the church to discover the multiple riches contained in the gospel? Perhaps these riches would not have come to light otherwise. Mankind must strive at unity through plurality, in the forms of thinking and acting of all cultures and civilizations. Might not such a manner of doing things be more consistent with the wisdom of God, his goodness, his providence?

Might this not also hold for interreligious dialogue? If so, it would, to some extent, coincide with the message of the Fifth Sura.

January 15, 2010

Last
(and Lasting)
Things

René Page died on February 2, 2010. He was eighty-six. His obituary did not appear in the *New York Times* or, as far as I know, in any other newspaper. He was little known outside the fraternities of Charles de Foucauld (1858–1916), those religious communities of men and women whose prayer and work lives are modeled on the "hidden" life of Jesus, that is, his life in Nazareth before his public ministry.

Page was born in Aubiers, a town in the west of France. At the age of sixteen, he entered the local minor seminary and later studied at the famed Saint Sulpice. But Page quickly realized that donning a cassock cut him off from others and upset his own natural spontaneity. This weighed heavily on him and he began to question his vocation to the priesthood. When he discovered the fraternities of Charles de Foucauld he recognized what he had been seeking: a consecrated life of prayer, lived among the poor, without privilege or status.

René made his novitiate with the Little Brothers of Jesus at El-Abiodh, in the Sahara, and took his first vows in October 1948 at the age of twenty-five. He spent the next two years with a small fraternity in Aix-en-Provence, where he worked on construction sites. This was followed by two years of additional theological studies at St. Maximin, interspersed with periods of work in the mines and in a textile factory.

It was apparent from the start to members of the fraternity that in René Page they had found someone special. He had a depth and a simplicity that the community needed, especially during the heady, chaotic postwar years, when postulants were arriving from all over the world and the number of local communities was multiplying. It was no coincidence that after René was ordained a priest in 1952, he was made provincial for France and Belgium. Later, in addition to this charge, he was asked to serve as novice master. René Voillaume, the founder of the Little Brothers of Jesus, eventually designated

Page his assistant prior, which made him the obvious choice for successor. When Voillaume resigned as prior in 1965 to found a new group, the Brothers of the Gospel, Page was chosen unanimously.

The style of the two Renés could hardly have been more different. René Voillaume was an iconic figure, the founder who defined the vision of the fraternity, an author whose books were widely read, and the only person in the fraternity called "Father." He was greatly admired and appreciated by the brothers, yet he seemed to belong to the universal church rather than to his religious community. In those days he was constantly on the move, giving conferences and retreats, visiting the different fraternities, and often spending more time with the hierarchy than with the brothers. In that foundational epoch, it could not have been otherwise. To survive and prosper, the fraternity had to be accepted by the official church. It was to this task that Voillaume tirelessly dedicated himself.

René Page was in his late forties when he was elected prior, but he looked like a teenager and didn't seem to take himself too seriously. He had a wry sense of humor and was a consummate storyteller. He also had a nervous tic and, for reasons I never knew, always wore dark glasses. Some have observed that he had the soul of a child. He was capable of suddenly being caught up in astonishment and admiration at the sight of a cloud formation or a meadow flower, and he could be scandalously indignant in the face of injustice or cruelty—as if he could not believe such malice possible in others. What most impressed me about René was the love he had for all of us in the community, a geographically scattered group of self-starters. That love manifested itself in very simple but unmistakable ways. With René there was never the least trace of superiority or condescension. Someone recently reminded me of the difference in context between the Sermon on the Mount in the Gospels of Matthew and Luke. In Matthew, Jesus "*went up* on a mountainside and sat down. His disciples *came to* him and he began to teach them..." In Luke, Jesus "*went down* with them and stood on a level place.... Then *raising his eyes to his disciples*, he said...." These differences seem to characterize the distinct styles of René Voillaume and René Page.

One Holy Thursday, a feast the brothers always celebrated together, Page performed the ritual washing of the feet. For him it was no mere ritual. He washed our feet with a joy and a passion that moved me to the core and gave me an intuition of what was in the heart of Jesus at the Last Supper. René was *always* there to serve; it was the reason for his existence.

On another occasion, I was passing through the Marseilles fraternity and had to catch an early-morning train to Paris. I got up around 4 a.m. and was trying to leave without disturbing the other brothers. René was already up and waiting for me. He insisted on accompanying me to the station and on carrying my bags. We shared many other adventures over the years, and we had our disagreements, but I always remained in awe of the man and never detected a false note in him.

René's respect for each member of the fraternity was a two-edged sword. It made it difficult for him to make personnel decisions, and it led him to assume others' problems as his own. I recall one occasion when I put myself in a very difficult position. After I informed René of the mess I'd created, he responded by saying *he* had not been sufficiently attentive; then he proceeded to assume all the blame. This habit eventually wore him down, and after his second six-year term as prior, he begged to be relieved of his responsibilities. Following that he spent several years in Paris, working first as a security guard and then as a mailman in a hospital—a job that put him at ease. He eventually moved to a fraternity near Toulouse, where he spent his latter years in semiretirement.

I once went to René for confession. When I had finished, he said quite simply that when we ask for the light of the Holy Spirit, we don't fully realize what we are asking for. This light, he said, is terrible and disorienting; it can destroy us. It is only "sweet" to authentic saints or to those who have no idea what they are talking about. For this light will reveal what we do not want revealed, tell us a truth we do not want to hear, and lead us where we do not want to go. This encounter revealed something of René's inner life to me. It challenged me then and still does. But in René's case it was also tragically prophetic—in a way I could not have imagined at the time.

In Toulouse, René's physical and mental health began to decline. He developed Alzheimer's, and this great temple of the Holy Spirit was physically and mentally emptied. It seemed as if the petition of the *Miserere*, "Do not withdraw your spirit from me," had simply been refused. To me, it was obscene, scandalous, that this gifted man, so full of the wisdom of God, had become a babbling idiot. Not only did the Holy Spirit appear to abandon him, other spirits invaded the premises. René, so compassionate and Christlike, began to exhibit fits of violence that were totally alien to him. Patients in the nursing home where he spent his last days characterized him as cruel—the last thing René would have tolerated in himself or in others. This shattering change troubled me deeply, and still does, years after his death.

It is not that I am unfamiliar with the ravages of Alzheimer's. My mother suffered from it, as did my mother-in-law, who lived with us for ten years. But René's case challenged me in a different way. True, I hadn't seen him in almost forty years and had only sporadic contact with him over much of that period. But René's words to me at the end of my confession had remained engraved in my memory. I also suspect that the quality and intensity of René's compassion for others somehow contributed to his illness. And then there is the matter of the communion of the saints: those mysterious affinities that link us to other persons, living and dead, with whom we share a distinct "quality" of grace. These individuals constitute the particular "crowd of witnesses" who sustain and encourage us, and whose destiny is somehow tied to our own.

It would be presumptuous, even indecent, of me to speculate on what went on between René and God during René's prolonged equivalent of "three days in the tomb." There are, however, certain points worth reflecting on. One of the members of the fraternity who cared for René during his final stages wrote: "Every illness which affects a person in what is most profound and most intimate is a form of evil in the world which is especially scandalous; it confronts us with a mystery we have to respect.... [René] also gave us enough signs to assure us that, alone in his [dark] night, he was before God and with God."

Modern medicine might explain René's deterioration as the result of damaged or diminished neurons; a psychologist might explain it as a manifestation of repressed instincts; a psychopathologist might understand the hostility observed in some mentally ill patients as the regression to a childhood state where one acts out uncontrollable emotional impulses. At one level, all these insights are valuable. But I believe such experiences can include other dimensions. The dynamics of grace and of evil can give "ordinary" experience another significance. While we cannot pretend to fully understand the dynamics, at times we sense there may be a deeper meaning than what science can tell us or we can initially grasp. The destruction of someone's unique personality, for example, strikes me as a manifestation of the mystery of evil. Sometimes the effects of evil or of grace in a person's life have nothing to do with the particular goodness or badness of the individual involved. And beyond that, even recognizing the reality of the powers of darkness does not mean we can clearly name or define them.

The Gospels attribute certain infirmities to the "devils." We must not take this lightly, for we confront a mystery here: evil in all its crudity and depth. In his final state, René Page seemed to be at the mercy of the Evil One, who mocked and destroyed him. In some sense, this is apparently where the Holy Spirit was leading him. I don't want to propose or accept an easy answer to this; a real scandal is involved here. Jesus likewise was led into the desert by the Spirit. After his baptism and forty-day fast, he was tempted by the Devil who, according to Luke, had a physical power over him, transporting him to a high mountain and even the pinnacle of the Temple, mocking him for his pretensions to be the Son of God, and then leaving him, only to return at a more opportune time. On the evening of his betrayal, Jesus foresaw that Peter would be at the mercy of the Evil One and prayed that Peter's faith would hold up. After the Resurrection, Jesus told Peter that in old age he would be led where he did not wish to go. In this, Peter would be following his master, the Wisdom and Word of God, the Giver of Life, who on the Cross was also taunted and physically destroyed. Through Jesus, God himself would become vulnerable.

Each year, the feast of Pentecost celebrates the outpouring of the Holy Spirit and the manifestation of the Spirit's gifts: peace and strength, light and joy, wisdom and discernment. But if the Spirit conforms us to Jesus, we will inevitably be led to the Cross, in one form or another. This is neither comforting nor guaranteed to edify. It may prove a humiliating experience, personally destructive and even scandalous. If the palpable gifts of the Spirit empower us to confront the manifestations of the "Mystery of Iniquity" and to cast out demons, they do not empower us to remain unscathed. For the only response given to the mystery of evil, the mystery of iniquity, is the one embodied in the crucified God. In a certain sense, we have to "give up the spirit" as Jesus did on the Cross. To pass to that other level, we will need to follow Jesus into the depths of hell.

"Live in hell and do not despair," advised Silouan, the holy elder of Mount Athos. The onset of late-stage Alzheimer's and the cruelty that René Page exhibited, so alien to all he represented and had lived, is perhaps analogous to the suffering of the giver of life himself, the pure one who "became sin" for us and destroyed death by assuming it from within. Where life has entered, death can no longer exist. For the Word remained united to the soulless body of Jesus in the tomb of Joseph of Arimathea and to the bodiless soul of Jesus in the depths of hell. Might not the suffering and diminishment of someone like René Page (and others whose mental faculties and habits of being abandon them) prove, in a paradoxical way, the path to that very purity of heart required for seeing God? Not only does God's mercy remain steadfast; his Spirit may be present to these broken ones in a different, more divine way—the Prayer within the prayer, the House within the house, the ineffable groanings of the Spirit above and beyond psychological experience.

We are in the throes of a great mystery here, one we cannot comprehend. René did not seek out his affliction any more than

Jesus sought his Cross. There are indeed truths we do not want to hear, pathways we do not wish to follow. In my more lucid moments, I'm almost *afraid* to invoke the Holy Spirit, for not all of us are called to participate in the redemption at certain levels. Still, those who *are* called, like René Page, are signs who remind us of the scandal of the Cross, a scandal we can never take seriously enough or fully grasp.

Confidence in the Resurrection is crucial here—the conviction that life is stronger than death, that life has in fact already triumphed over death, that, in spite of appearances, there is a glory yet to be fully revealed and understood. Were it not so, God would be a monster. But God is our surest companion.

May 18, 2012

ONE OF THE LEAST

I could see it coming. For many years I had worked at demanding and dangerous jobs as a Little Brother of Jesus: more than a decade in foundry work, a few years of lumberjacking, a stint in a brick factory. This was partly by choice. I wanted to take the last place, as Jesus did, to do the jobs nobody wanted to do in solidarity with the oppressed. But most of the time that was my only option anyway since I was living abroad and could get a work permit only for the jobs the "natives" didn't want. When I returned to the United States I was already in my forties. I took a custodial job at the New England Aquarium in Boston and worked there for the next thirty-three years.

But suddenly the years began to take their toll. I was unsteady on my feet. At the end of a shift at work, I was exhausted, almost sleepwalking. And it was precisely at the end of a shift, when I was taking out the last load of trash, that I fell down a couple of steps and wound up with a broken hip and wrist. At the age of seventy-seven you don't just bounce back from something like that. From now on, my balance will always be precarious. The hip will remain sore, and the wrist will continue to bother me. There's no chance of my returning to my job at the aquarium. I've become a kind of handicapped person. It's a whole different ballgame now.

The transition has not gone very smoothly. I have always been fiercely independent and now need others' help with things both big and small. I'd always seen myself as a champion for the underdog, the useless and the helpless, throwing in my lot with them and defending them as well as I could. In my more lucid moments, this was because they were a presence of Jesus for me and I hoped that somehow, however awkwardly and almost in spite of myself, I represented a certain presence of Jesus for them. Did I see myself as some kind of hero stooping down to the poor? Well, yes—a little bit at the beginning maybe. But I soon discovered that I had much to learn from the patience, generosity, and good humor of my neighbors and coworkers.

Now I'm the one others must stoop down to help. I'm the one who's useless, limited, and dependent, often cranky and frustrated to boot. But I've also discovered something else: the goodness and kindness of people toward me. Not just my friends, my neighbors, and old coworkers, but pretty much everyone. Total strangers will go out of their way to assist me, demonstrating spontaneous compassion toward this wreck of a human being wandering the streets. It has occurred to me that when people do such things for me, they are really doing them for Jesus, even though they most likely never think of that. The Gospel of St. Matthew tells us that Jesus will gather all mankind at the Last Judgment and judge each according to his or her charity toward the least, for whatever act is done or not done for them concerns Jesus personally. So in this broken person that I have become, I'm also an occasion for people to help Jesus and thus secure eternal life in his kingdom. This is something I never could have accomplished otherwise. It is a silent yet real mystery. It sometimes strikes me as very wonderful. I'd never imagined myself becoming a presence of Jesus in this way.

This is all the more humbling since I myself used to be tempted to look away from the aged and the infirm. I thought I had all the answers then, looking in from the outside. But when you are stripped of everything that constituted your life, all these answers seem absurd, arrogant, even obscene. There is the tenderness of the Trinity playing itself out on another level. A strange Paradise, promised to the Good Thief simply for hanging on a cross next to Jesus—not as an innocent but as someone who knew he deserved his humiliation. It can be presumed that the Good Thief was buried not far from Jesus. Yet Scripture tells us it was precisely on that day—not the next—that he was remembered in the Kingdom.

February 20, 2015

HE DOES NOT FORGET

Now that I am no longer capable of the kind of manual labor I used to do for a living, I have fallen back on translating and proofreading work as an excuse to justify my existence. A while back I was translating some French newsletters from the Little Brothers of Jesus and came across one that hit very close to home. It was from an elderly brother in Africa who had done hard physical work all of his life. Now, in his old age, he was unable to do that kind of work. He took this to be a call to focus more on prayer and, above all, to intercede for all the people he had known and loved. But there, too, he had problems. There were so many whose names he had forgotten; his memories of past events and interactions had become muddled and confused. He felt ungrateful and even guilty for relations he had not fostered.

I recognized myself all too well in what he wrote. I have lost contact with so many people who meant a lot to me at different stages of my life, people I loved dearly and really cared for and who had given me so much and made me what I am. But this brother in Africa went on, adding a reflection that was, he said, the source of his peace and that opened a door to mine. We might forget these people from our past, but God does not. He does not forget that we once loved them and prayed for them, and his memory of that is eternal, as is the reality of our prayer.

I think it was Raïssa Maritain who, in her book *We Have Been Friends Together*, looks back at all the projects she and her friends had that never came to anything. She does so with gratitude, for, as she notes, the Holy Spirit is at work not only in the works that last for centuries but also in all our little failures, which appear to have no tomorrow. These too, in whatever they had of purity and love, will live forever, discreetly, and will, in their own way, shape the church.

Another newsletter, another brother—this one writing from a nursing home in Chile, which he had entered a few months earlier. He had suffered a debilitating stroke nearly twenty years ago. Since then, two other Little Brothers of Jesus in Chile looked after him. Now they too were growing old, and he realized that he was becoming too much of a burden for them. It was his decision to enter the nursing home. He was very touched by the people who work there and the volunteers who simply try to support the elderly. For, as he goes on to say, "the world of the elderly holds no special attraction. The elderly show humanity in its poorest state, having lost all power of seduction, seemingly reduced to waiting for whatever will happen, with little interest, a silent and somewhat drowsy wait."

When he chose these elderly as his companions for the rest of his life, he thought it was essential to feel some of the affection Jesus has for them and not just "get along" with them. He cites the gospel passage where we are told that Jesus gave thanks to his Father for having taught him how to enrich us with his poverty, for the way in which the Kingdom of God is established by the poor and the humble. "The people in this nursing home are the bearers of humanity's profound poverty and they are the living guardians of theological hope. These are the places from which the prayers of the poor rise up to the Father because they are accompanied by their lives, their tiredness, their drudgery, their helplessness, their poverty." The brother concludes that God wants him to join them, to receive from them, to learn from them. Christ, the Power and Wisdom of God, chose what was common and contemptible in this world, including the apparent tedium of old age, to reduce to nothing all that seems so important to us, including youth and physical beauty. This brother sees himself as another old man who can share with these people their hope in God's revelation, waiting, patiently and prayerfully, for "whatever will happen" in the fullness of time.

May 4, 2018

Joseph Cunneen, a longtime contributor to *Commonweal*, passed away in his sleep on July 29, 2012. He was eighty-nine years old. The son of an attorney and a teacher, Joe attended the College of the Holy Cross in Worcester, Massachusetts, and served in France with the 101st division of Combat Engineers during World War II. It was there he discovered the theological renewal that would flourish in the postwar years and ultimately lead to Vatican II. This *nouvelle théologie* was very different from the theology to which he had been exposed in college, which was mainly a kind of apologetics.

In 1950, Joe founded a quarterly magazine, *CrossCurrents*, whose purpose was to introduce American Catholics to the new theological developments in Europe. The magazine published the work of people like Yves Congar, Henri de Lubac, and Jean-Guenolé-Marie Danielou, and many of the articles were translated into English by Joe himself. During the early years of *CrossCurrents*, the main editorial office was Joe's garage. His staff consisted of his wife, Sally, a writer and teacher who supported Joe wholeheartedly. In the early days, he would write out the addresses for each copy of *CrossCurrents* by hand, pile the magazines into his car, and deliver them to the local post office. *CrossCurrents* would become an important point of reference in the evolution of American Catholicism. Thomas Merton was especially supportive of the work Joe was doing. Meanwhile, to make ends meet, Joe taught courses on cinema at several universities, while Sally worked as an English teacher at Rockland Community College. Eventually Joe came to realize that *CrossCurrents* would need some sort of sponsor in order to survive. After exploring his options, he finally decided to associate the magazine with the Association for Religious and Intellectual Life, which had its seat at the College of New Rochelle. The Association provided resources for *CrossCurrents*, but it also had a broader agenda of its own, which was somewhat different from Joe's. He continued on as one of the editors, and

Sally remained on the editorial staff, but they were no longer the decision makers.

It was at this point that I first got to know Joe. I had happened upon an early issue of *CrossCurrents* while I was doing theological studies in Washington, D.C., in the 1950s. Like the theology Joe had been exposed to at Holy Cross, the formation I was receiving was mainly an extension of the catechism, with loaded questions and easy answers. *CrossCurrents* questioned the questions, and, instead of supplying easy answers, it invited the reader into the mysteries of the faith. The new perspectives it offered had an important effect on some of the big decisions I would make. Many years later, never having published anything before, I submitted an article to *CrossCurrents* on a lark. I was surprised to receive a long and very encouraging letter from Joe. He would have liked to use it, he said, but he was no longer "in charge" at *CrossCurrents* and had been overruled. Shortly after this exchange, Joe came all the way up to Boston to meet me, and we spent a couple of days together. We hit it off at once; it was as if we had always known each other. This moved me very deeply. I was a nobody, a custodian at the New England Aquarium, and Joe was—in my eyes—a major figure in American Catholicism. Thus began a wonderful friendship. I went to New York several times to visit Joe and Sally, who received me with a disarming simplicity and made me feel like one of the family.

Eventually Joe retired from *CrossCurrents* and dedicated himself to translating and promoting the works of the French writer Jean Sulivan—a project that met with little success. For many years, he was the *National Catholic Reporter*'s film critic, and published a book on the director Robert Bresson. Both he and Sally continued to contribute to magazines such as *Commonweal, America*, and *Spirit*.

The last time I saw Joe was at the Catholic Worker's seventy-fifth-birthday celebration in New York. Sally was recuperating from breast cancer and had to follow a strict and exquisitely insipid diet. Out of solidarity, Joe followed the same culinary regime—until he became anemic and started to have fainting spells. At night, he would read Sally to sleep, no matter how much time it took.

The relationship between Joe and Sally was not just lovey-dovey: I witnessed several occasions when they didn't see eye to eye or got on each other's nerves. Yet the tensions almost immediately receded into the background of their deep love. This made a lasting impression on me. When Sally died, I tried to keep in touch with Joe but he rarely replied. When he did, it was with only a sentence or two. His last email to me, sent a few months before his death, simply informed me that he was entering a nursing home.

Joe was not an original thinker. He was what the French would call a *passeur*—a "ferryman," literally: someone who channels other people's ideas, and this he did with enthusiasm, dedication, and self-effacement. He had absolutely no pretensions; he was an open book. He was aware of all the good he had done and equally aware of his failures. He would speak of both in the same tone. We should be grateful to him not just because of what he did but also because of what he was: a true Israelite, without guile.

September 28, 2012

A SECOND DEATH

I might imagine the dead waking, dazed into a shadowless light in which they know themselves altogether for the first time. It is a light that is merciless until they accept its mercy; by it, they are at once condemned and redeemed. It is Hell until it is Heaven. Seeing themselves in that light, if they are willing, they see how far they have failed the only justice of loving one another; it punishes them with their own judgment. And yet, in suffering the light's awful clarity, in seeing themselves within it, they see its forgiveness and its beauty and are consoled.

—Wendell Berry, *A World Lost*

I turned eighty-two not long ago. According to popular mythology, with age comes wisdom. That might be true for some, but for me the years have brought forgetfulness and confusion. My silence is not the profound silence of an elder who has arrived, after a long life, at a sort of synthesis; it stems more from a fear of saying something really stupid about things I've forgotten or only vaguely remember.

Another aspect of aging is the realization that things are going to change radically for me pretty soon. I'm both curious about dying and afraid of all the uncertainty that surrounds it. That is why the above passage from one of Wendell Berry's novels hit home so hard. It seemed to me a very beautiful and coherent description of Purgatory—something we don't often talk about anymore.

One of the major difficulties we have in trying to imagine the afterlife is that it is outside of time as we know it—for time is linked to material change. We say that there is "no time" in God who is an Eternal Instant. The theologians tell us that the "spiritual time" of the disembodied soul is something beyond what we can imagine, since we can imagine time only as a succession of "states," with a before and after.

There are those who imagine we will all experience an instantaneous bodily resurrection at the moment of our deaths because, whatever the historical moment at which we die, there is no delay in our experience of this "spiritual time" between the moment of death and the Parousia. The judgment of each person would thus be integrated within the fulfillment of all things. All that was hidden would be revealed *all at once*, rather than one person at a time. The mystical links that bind us together with earlier and later generations would be part of this general revelation, all of us, our ancestors and our posterity, meeting in an eternal present in which we would discover both a crucifying truth and an ineffable mercy. This all-encompassing revelation would constitute the essential joy of the blessed.

But that would seem to leave something out. In the Apostle's Creed we proclaim that, after his death, Christ descended into Hell. For Urs von Balthasar, the disembodied soul of Christ continues to be united to the Word of God but no longer experiences this union during the "three days in the tomb." Hell is the place where there is neither faith nor hope nor love. This is sin in its essence, a "second death" in which we experience the absence of God and thus a meaninglessness without light. Here, too, all sense of time is lost, so that the Resurrection comes as an abrupt surprise.

If we are to follow Christ, we, in our turn, must go where he went. We must experience those dark corners and hidden horrors in our soul that we did not dare to explore, and that God's mercy has until then kept in obscurity. Then we shall realize that when we acquiesced to evil in our choices, we ratified evil in itself. But it is also precisely when we enter into this abyss that we will find Jesus "trampling down death by death and upon those in the tombs bestowing life." For the "three days in the tomb" represent the victory of life over death by the entry of Life *into* death. Life destroys death from within. When we, following Jesus, enter into death, we will find him there. This is what Wendell Berry seems to mean when he says that we must descend into hell until it becomes heaven. We must accept the merciless light until it becomes mercy, be punished by our own enlightened judgment in order to receive a mercy beyond imagination. When St. Thomas, in his *Summa Theologica*, asks if it was fitting that Christ die on the cross, his first answer was that

Jesus did so in order that we might not be afraid to die, to die even a horrendous death. All this, in the end, is a mystery where we can only babble, guess, hope—and, yes, fear a little too.

March 2020

REAL AND UNIMAGINABLE

Many years ago, I worked for several months as a gravedigger in the Catholic cemetery of Leeds, England. The grounds crew consisted of a man named Denis, his three sons, and myself. Denis resented me. I wasn't his son. I wasn't even from Yorkshire. For all he knew, I could be a CIA agent out to get him. The superintendent of the cemetery was, believe it or not, a guy by the name of Ted Graves. He was separated from his wife and lived in a little house in the middle of the cemetery with his teenaged daughter. Mr. Graves was a man of prayer who tried to live the Gospel and who dabbled in philosophy. He was also totally impractical and absentminded. On several occasions when we'd be sitting around or tinkering with something, a procession would suddenly show up at the gate. Mr. Graves had forgotten another burial. Denis was a master at coping with situations like this. He'd lead the procession in circles around the cemetery for about half an hour while the rest of us would frantically dig. There was a way of hanging the artificial grass carpet over the sides of the grave to make the hole look deeper than it actually was. During my stint we pulled this off more than once and got away with it.

In the family plots in England at that time, you didn't pour concrete over a buried casket. You just threw dirt on it. So when a grave was reopened to greet another family member, you dug until you reached the first casket—and there was an anxious moment when you would find out whether or not it supported your weight. Some parts of the cemetery were very humid and hilly. Which meant that the coffins in those sectors tended to rot. The worst possible scenario was a "re-opener" on a slope in the humid section. Perfect joy is standing in the rain in a ten-foot hole, your foot having gone through the rotten casket you're standing on, and watching the caskets in the next grave uphill slowly sliding through the mud above your head.

Denis once summed up the fruits of his experience quite succinctly: "No way these piles of shit are coming back up."

On the face of things, such as we saw them, this was a perfectly obvious conclusion.

A while back I read in a survey of religious beliefs that only a minority of Christians believed in a physical resurrection, be it Christ's or ours. This is nothing new. The Athenians laughed at St. Paul when he broached the subject (see Acts 17:16–34). His Corinthian converts had trouble accepting the Resurrection in spite of Paul's personal testimony of his encounter with the risen Christ on the road to Damascus and the report of other witnesses who were still alive. In our own enlightened age, this core belief of Christianity appears irreconcilable with both rationality and experience.

"How are the dead to be raised up? What kind of body will they have?" (1 Corinthians 15:35). St. Paul's reaction to these legitimate questions isn't very diplomatic. "What a stupid question" is the essence of his reply. He goes on to explain to us dummies that the corruptible body is the seed of an incorruptible body, the natural body the seed of a spiritual body. As if that should be obvious. It might have been to Paul, who experienced the third heaven, but for those of us who have not received such lights, the idea of a "spiritual body" is a very nebulous and enigmatic concept.

How, then, should we envisage resurrection? Scripture and tradition affirm the physical resurrection of Jesus as the model and prototype of ours. I don't think that there is any getting around the fact that, notwithstanding all our postmodern deconstructionism, this is a core belief of Christianity. Our points of reference should be the postpaschal accounts of the risen Jesus and his preliminary glorification on Mount Tabor.

In the gospel accounts of the manifestations of the risen Christ, there are consistencies and inconsistencies. He is not immediately recognized in certain of these narratives—on the road to Emmaus, on the shore of Lake Tiberias, in the garden of the tomb. He invites Thomas to feel his wounds yet forbids Mary Magdalene to touch him. Many of the meetings between the Resurrection and the Ascension include a shared meal. If the angelic witnesses of the Resurrection appear in their glory and inspire fear, the risen Jesus does not. He exudes a sense of peace, fulfillment, and total domination, yet he is discreet and fraternal. He bears the marks of his Passion. He passes through closed doors.

It is the same Jesus, the King of the Jews who hung on the cross. Yet he is also somehow different. Something has changed. He is still in this world but no longer subject to its laws. There is also something incomplete about him during the forty pascal days. He has not yet returned to his Father. He has not yet manifested the fullness of his victory over death, which will be revealed only "when he comes again in glory," and this will be accompanied by the resurrection of all and the glorification of the Mystical Body of Christ. The evangelists' descriptions of the resurrected Christ give us a glimpse at a new dimension of existence, but they also give the impression that much more remains concealed than has been revealed.

So should we just let it go at that, and stop asking what Paul called stupid questions? I don't think so. The apparent contradiction between the divine promise and what we know about the body needs to be addressed.

Much can be learned, I believe, from the epiphany on Mount Tabor. Jesus is with Moses and Elias in the splendor of his glorified humanity, and they converse about his approaching passion and death. This is not the resurrected Christ of the forty days whose glory still isn't manifested because he has not yet returned to the Father. This is Jesus in his triumphal resplendence. Here time touches eternity. They who had experienced the divine glory on Sinai (Moses) and Horeb (Elias), are both visibly present on the holy mountain along with Jesus and are recognized by Peter, James, and John. Their physical presence is so real that Peter suggests erecting tents for them. They appear in the midst of a cloud that the Fathers of the Church identified as the Holy Spirit. All this is before Christ "comes again in glory," before his ascension and resurrection, his passion and death. And yet to the chosen disciples who saw him on Mount Tabor, his visible glory that day was as much as they could bear. The Transfiguration prefigured all that the general resurrection will finally reveal.

Tabor reveals Christ as a mediator between time and eternity. The very structure of the Incarnation implies the entrance of eternity into time and time into eternity. The Incarnation refers temporal realities to a dimension beyond themselves where they acquire their full meaning. To enter into eternity is to enter into one's true identity, and the body is essential to our identity—so much so that, for St. Thomas, a disembodied soul would not really be a person: the very nature of the soul is to be the form of the body.

There must be a continuity between the bodies we have now and the spiritual body to which Paul refers. The spiritual body is our present body fulfilled according to the will of Christ. Despite its infirmities and imperfections, our present body is destined to become the body of a child of God. This does not necessarily imply that all the elements of that body will be identical with the elements of the bodies we have now. But then, the bodies we have now are not identical with the bodies we had a few years ago. We know from modern biology that our physical components are constantly changing, our cells constantly being replaced, yet the soul remains the same and makes these elements ours.

Finally, it is worth noting that on Mount Tabor, it is not only the visage of Christ that becomes brighter than the sun; his clothes, too, shine forth in dazzling splendor and the mountain is covered with a luminous cloud like that of the Exodus. The glory of Christ extends to the material world around him. So, in some mysterious way, will the glory of the spiritual body radiate and transform the new heavens and the new earth. Indeed, the whole created universe will be freed from its slavery to corruption and share in the glorious freedom of the children of God.

The Father without beginning and the consubstantial Spirit are present on Tabor, as they were in the waters of the Jordan when Jesus was baptized. In both instances, the voice of the Father confirms his love for his Son. On Tabor the Spirit manifests itself not in the form of a dove, but as a luminous and transforming cloud. It is the Spirit who fills all things with life, gently and forcefully, as the Advent antiphon sings. It is the Spirit who glorifies the humanity of Christ and, through him, all of creation.

So my friend Denis was wrong. Strange as it sounds—and impossible as it may be for us to imagine now—at the end of time it's all coming back up. Until then, all Creation groans.

May 5, 2017

THE FEAR OF GOD

The only physical experience I've ever had of the "supernatural" occurred during Dorothy Day's funeral Mass. When the gospel reading began, I saw sparks coming from Dorothy's coffin. My first thought was that there was a short circuit somewhere, but no one seemed concerned. Once the gospel reading was over, the sparks stopped. I dared not mention it to anyone at the time, and no one commented on it. It took me years to muster up the courage to ask my friend Patrick Jordan if he had noticed anything unusual at the funeral. He hadn't. When I told him of my experience, he said quite simply, "That was for you." There it was: a gift, a reassuring vision, and my only reaction had been fear and shame.

Maybe my fear was something like that of the myrrh-bearing women on the day of the Resurrection. Initially they dared not tell anyone that they had seen an angel proclaiming that Jesus had been raised. Later, when the Risen Christ first appeared to his apostles, they were afraid and confused and thought that they were seeing a ghost. Maybe they were afflicted with a type of fear that haunts us all to one degree or another: the fear that the Christian narrative is simply too good to be true.

The fear of the Lord is a theme that runs throughout the Old Testament. It is called the beginning of wisdom and defines the just man. Yet the risen Christ tells his disciples not to be afraid and transforms their fear into joy. When I was a boy, we learned in catechism class that the God of the Old Testament was a jealous and often angry God, whereas Jesus appeased his anger and revealed him to be a loving Father. We don't talk that way anymore. We know it is the same God who reveals Himself in the Old Testament and the New. But the fact that one of the Holy Trinity became flesh and dwelt among us manifests a depth and quality of love we could never have imagined. It took centuries before the church was able to articulate the immensity of this gift, and this is still an ongoing process. With the New Testament revelation, the accent shifts to the "perfect love that casts out fear" (1 John 5:18). Nonetheless, even with its subordinated importance, fear of the Lord remains part of the church's legacy as one of the gifts of the Holy Spirit.

When we speak of the fear of God, everything depends on what we are afraid of and why. Classical spirituality distinguishes between servile fear and filial fear. Both suppose faith and grace. Servile fear is the fear of punishment, and the greatest punishment imaginable is the eternal loss of God. God is all-merciful, but we have to accept this mercy and be aware that we are in need of it. Filial fear would be the fear a son has of offending a loving father to whom he owes everything. In the gospels, God reveals himself as a father, a father to Jesus and a father to us all. Charles Péguy wrote that "all the sentiments, all the movements that we should have for God, God first had them for us." In some mysterious, analogical way, the father is afraid—afraid of losing us. And so he sends his son.

Hope and faith will pass; love and awe will not. In heaven, there will no longer be fear of losing or offending God. When all has been made manifest, there will only be gratitude, security, and an ever-increasing love. Then our fear will take the form of an awe constantly purified and enriched. But this awe is already present in this life in an inchoate and imperfect state. Here, God's unknown dimensions themselves become a source of joy, a constant anticipation of a yet greater joy.

There is a passage in Dostoevsky's *Crime and Punishment* that always moves me deeply. Marmeladov, a self-loathing and self-sabotaging alcoholic, gives a drunken speech in which he imagines the Last Judgment:

> And he will judge and forgive them all, the good and the evil, the wise and the meek. And when he has done with all of them, then will he summon us. "You too come forth ye drunkards, come forth ye weak ones, come forth ye children of shame." And we shall all come forth without shame and shall stand before him. And he will say to us: "You are swine made in the image of the beast and with his mark. But come ye also." And the wise ones and those of understanding will say: "O Lord, why dost thou receive these men?" And he will say: "This is

why I receive them, O ye of understanding. Not one of them believed himself to be worthy of this!" And he shall hold out his hands to us and we shall fall down before him…and we shall weep…and we shall understand all things and all will be understood.

All things: the things hidden to us now will be revealed, to our relief or bewilderment; and the things about each one of us that were invisible to others will be revealed. We will no longer be alone with the deep realities—including the deep wounds—that we cannot communicate in this world.

September 12, 2014

A COMMUNION OF SINNERS AND SAINTS

I have no idea what, exactly, the Beatific Vision will be like. I cannot begin to imagine it. I can only desire it as a "mystery gift," a vague promise of something far beyond my experience. What I can imagine and look forward to is the revelation of what we call the "communion of the saints," this mysterious intertwining of destinies, our solidarity in salvation. In the Creed, our profession of the communion of the saints is followed by the affirmation of our belief in the forgiveness of sins, the resurrection of the dead, and life everlasting. I think that these all go together.

But before becoming a communion of saints we are first of all a communion of sinners. There is a sense of solidarity even in sin—a sense that, in making a pact with the evil within us, we make a pact with evil itself and thus become responsible for the sins of all—from the blood of Abel to the apostasy of the last apostate. To refuse this solidarity is, in itself, a sin against communion. We are asked to carry one another's burdens, including the burden of sin, and thus fulfill the law of Christ, who, being sinless, could assume all sin without being consumed by it. Of course, being sinners, we can do this only imperfectly. Sometimes our own burden of sin may seem like burden enough. But so long as we are members of one body, we cannot forget the other members. As St. Paul says in 1 Corinthians 12:26, "If one member suffers, all the members suffer with it."

The other side of this coin is that "when one member is honored, all the members share its joy." And when one member is pardoned, it affects the whole Mystical Body of Christ. Pardon is not a purely individual experience. By receiving mercy we become more merciful ourselves; the communion of saints is the communion of those who have become vessels of mercy. In *The City of God*, St. Augustine writes that "our righteousness in this life consists rather in the pardoning of sins than in the perfection of virtue." When Jesus first appeared to his disciples after the Resurrection, he breathed on them his Holy Spirit and empowered them to forgive sins (John 20:19–23). Ever since then, the pardon of sins has remained an essential element of the pilgrim church's mission, and it will always be linked to the resurrection of the dead, as it was on that first evening. The pardon of every sinner contributes to the general resurrection, to the death of death.

But mercy is not simply the forgiveness of sins. It is a participation in the very Holiness of God. The Kingdom of the Father is a household where all is held in common. St. Augustine has this remarkable comment: "Love is a powerful thing, my brothers and sisters. Do you wish to see how powerful love is? Whoever, through some necessity, cannot accomplish what God commands, let him love the one who accomplishes it and he accomplishes it in that other."

We are told that there are many rooms in the Father's house, but I doubt if they are all single-occupancy. I believe that, within the communion of saints, there are affinities of grace, that each of us is surrounded by a particular cloud of witnesses, whose quality of grace is in some mysterious way related to our own. Some of these witnesses are known to us; others are not. What I do hope to find in the Father's house—and try to imagine—is the restoration of all that is beautiful and pure in people and in their works, the fulfillment of old friendships known and the discovery of the discrete links that have made my own joy possible. That would indeed be life everlasting.

February 23, 2018

CPSIA information can be obtained
at www.ICGtesting.com
Printed in the USA
BVHW040743080221
599618BV00016B/1119